Building RESTful Web Services with Spring 5
Second Edition

Leverage the power of Spring 5.0, Java SE 9, and Spring Boot 2.0

Raja CSP Raman
Ludovic Dewailly

BIRMINGHAM - MUMBAI

Building RESTful Web Services with Spring 5
Second Edition

Copyright © 2018 Packt Publishing

All rights reserved. No part of this book may be reproduced, stored in a retrieval system, or transmitted in any form or by any means, without the prior written permission of the publisher, except in the case of brief quotations embedded in critical articles or reviews.

Every effort has been made in the preparation of this book to ensure the accuracy of the information presented. However, the information contained in this book is sold without warranty, either express or implied. Neither the authors, nor Packt Publishing or its dealers and distributors, will be held liable for any damages caused or alleged to have been caused directly or indirectly by this book.

Packt Publishing has endeavored to provide trademark information about all of the companies and products mentioned in this book by the appropriate use of capitals. However, Packt Publishing cannot guarantee the accuracy of this information.

Commissioning Editor: Aaron Lazar
Acquisition Editor: Chaitanya Nair
Content Development Editor: Zeeyan Pinheiro
Technical Editor: Romy Dias
Copy Editor: Safis Editing
Project Coordinator: Vaidehi Sawant
Proofreader: Safis Editing
Indexer: Rekha Nair
Graphics: Jason Monteiro
Production Coordinator: Shantanu Zagade

First published: October 2015
Second edition: January 2018

Production reference: 1230118

Published by Packt Publishing Ltd.
Livery Place
35 Livery Street
Birmingham
B3 2PB, UK.

ISBN 978-1-78847-589-1

www.packtpub.com

To my parents, Raman and Gandhi, for their great support through my tough times and for nurturing me to be prepared for whatever challenges come my way. To my brother and sister for their wishes and guidance throughout my life.

– Raja CSP Raman

`mapt.io`

Mapt is an online digital library that gives you full access to over 5,000 books and videos, as well as industry leading tools to help you plan your personal development and advance your career. For more information, please visit our website.

Why subscribe?

- Spend less time learning and more time coding with practical eBooks and Videos from over 4,000 industry professionals

- Improve your learning with Skill Plans built especially for you

- Get a free eBook or video every month

- Mapt is fully searchable

- Copy and paste, print, and bookmark content

PacktPub.com

Did you know that Packt offers eBook versions of every book published, with PDF and ePub files available? You can upgrade to the eBook version at `www.PacktPub.com` and as a print book customer, you are entitled to a discount on the eBook copy. Get in touch with us at `service@packtpub.com` for more details.

At `www.PacktPub.com`, you can also read a collection of free technical articles, sign up for a range of free newsletters, and receive exclusive discounts and offers on Packt books and eBooks.

Contributors

About the authors

Raja CSP Raman has been a software developer for 13 years and is the founder of TalentAccurate, an IT skills validation tool that helps start-ups and small companies filter candidates without going through their resume. He also founded Pointopedia, a website that provides 15 lines of information on any topic, without any images or links. Raja likes photography and watching documentaries on history and science.

> I'd like to thank my parents, brother, and sister, who guided and encouraged me to write this book.
>
> Also, I'd like to thank my TCE (Thiagarajar College of Engineering) classmates who inspired me and helped me focus on my vision.
>
> I especially thank Zeeyan, Romy, and other editors for their wonderful guidance throughout this book! Without them, I wouldn't have done it.

Ludovic Dewailly is a senior, hands-on software engineer and development manager with over 12 years of experience in designing and building software solutions on platforms ranging from resource-constrained mobile devices to cloud computing systems. He is currently helping FancyGiving (a social shopping, wishing, and gifting platform) with designing and building their system. Ludovic's interests lie in software architecture and tackling web scale challenges.

About the reviewer

Glenn De Paula is a graduate of the University of the Philippines Integrated School and is a computer science graduate from the University of the Philippines. He has 12 years of industry experience, in the government's ICT institute and the banking industry.

He uses Spring, Grails, and JavaScript for his day-to-day activities. He has developed numerous Java web applications for the government and has been the team leader on several projects.

He is consistently involved in systems analysis and design, source code review, testing, implementation, training, and mentoring.

> *I would like to thank the author of this book, the editors, and our publisher, Packt Publishing, for giving me this opportunity.*
>
> *I would also like to thank my managers and supervisors for mentoring me and trusting me with projects that helped improve my career.*
>
> *A big thank you to my family and friends for all the support. Especially, I thank my wife, Elaine, for all the love and patience.*

Packt is searching for authors like you

If you're interested in becoming an author for Packt, please visit `authors.packtpub.com` and apply today. We have worked with thousands of developers and tech professionals, just like you, to help them share their insight with the global tech community. You can make a general application, apply for a specific hot topic that we are recruiting an author for, or submit your own idea.

Table of Contents

Preface — 1
Chapter 1: A Few Basics — 7
    REST – a basic understanding — 8
        Uniform interface — 8
        Client and server — 8
        Stateless — 8
        Cacheable — 9
        Layered system — 9
        Code on demand (COD) — 9
        More on REST — 10
    Imperative and Reactive programming — 10
        Reactive Streams — 11
        Benefits of Reactive programming — 11
    Reactive programming in Java and Spring 5 — 12
    Our RESTful web service architecture — 12
    Summary — 14
Chapter 2: Building RESTful Web Services in Spring 5 with Maven — 15
    Apache Maven — 15
        Creating a project with Maven — 17
            Viewing a POM file after creating a project — 17
        POM file structure — 18
        Understanding POM dependencies — 19
        Adding Log4j 2.9.1 to POM dependency — 20
            Dependency trees — 22
            Spring Boot — 24
    Developing RESTful web services — 24
        Creating a project base — 24
        Working with your favorite IDE — 26
    Summary — 32
Chapter 3: Flux and Mono (Reactor Support) in Spring — 33
    Benefits of Reactive programming — 33
        Reactive Core and Streams — 34
            Back pressures and Reactive Streams — 35
            WebFlux — 35

Table of Contents

        Basic REST API   36
        Flux   36
        Mono   37
   User class with Reactive – REST   37
   Summary   45

Chapter 4: CRUD Operations in Spring REST   47

   CRUD operations in Spring REST   47
      HTTP methods   48
      Reactive server initialization   49
      Sample values in the repository   50
      getAllUsers – mapping   51
      getAllUsers – implementation in the handler and repository   52
      Testing the endpoint – getAllUsers   53
      getUser – implementation in the handler and repository   54
      Testing the endpoint – getUser   56
      createUser – implementation in the handler and repository   56
      Testing the endpoint – createUser   57
      updateUser – implementation in the handler and repository   58
      Testing the endpoint – updateUser   60
      deleteUser – implementation in the handler and repository   61
      Testing the endpoint – deleteUser   62
   Summary   63

Chapter 5: CRUD Operations in Plain REST (Without Reactive) and File Upload   65

   Mapping CRUD operations to HTTP methods   66
   Creating resources   66
   CRUD operation in Spring 5 (without Reactive)   71
      getAllUsers – implementation   73
      getUser – implementation   75
      createUser – implementation   76
      updateUser – implementation   78
      deleteUser – implementation   80
   File uploads – REST API   80
      Testing the file upload   83
   Summary   83

Chapter 6: Spring Security and JWT (JSON Web Token)   85

   Spring Security   85
      Authentication and authorization   86

JSON Web Token (JWT)	86
JWT dependency	86
Creating a JWT token	87
Generating a token	89
Getting a subject from a JWT token	90
Getting a subject from a token	91
Summary	**91**
Chapter 7: Testing RESTful Web Services	**93**
JUnit	**93**
MockMvc	**94**
Testing a single user	95
Postman	**97**
Getting all the users – Postman	97
Adding a user – Postman	98
Generating a JWT – Postman	99
Getting the subject from the token	99
SoapUI	**100**
Getting all the users – SoapUI	101
Generating JWT SoapUI	102
Getting the subject from the token – SoapUI	103
jsoup	**104**
Getting a user – jsoup	106
Adding a user – jsoup	107
Running the test cases	108
Summary	**108**
Chapter 8: Performance	**109**
HTTP compression	**109**
Content negotiation	110
Accept-Encoding	110
Content-Encoding	111
Server-driven content negotiation	111
Agent-driven content negotiation	112
HTTP caching	**112**
HTTP cache control	112
Public caching	112
Private caching	113
No-cache	113
Only-if-cached	114
Cache validation	115
ETags	115

Table of Contents

Last-Modified/If-Modified-Since headers	115
Cache implementation	**116**
The REST resource	116
Caching with ETags	121
Summary	**124**

Chapter 9: AOP and Logger Controls — 125

Aspect-oriented programming (AOP)	**125**
AOP (@Before) with execution	126
Testing AOP @Before execution	127
AOP (@Before) with annotation	127
Testing AOP @Before annotation	129
Integrating AOP with JWT	129
Logger controls	**132**
SLF4J, Log4J, and Logback	132
Logback framework	132
Logback dependency and configuration	133
Logging levels	134
Logback implementation in class	134
Summary	**136**

Chapter 10: Building a REST Client and Error Handling — 137

Building a REST client	**137**
RestTemplate	138
Error handling	**141**
Customized exception	143
Summary	**143**

Chapter 11: Scaling — 145

Clustering	**145**
Benefits of clustering	146
Load balancing	**146**
Scaling databases	**147**
Vertical scaling	147
Horizontal scaling	147
Read replicas	147
Pool connections	148
Use multiple masters	148
Load balancing in DB servers	148
Database partitioning	148
Sharding (horizontal partitioning)	149
Vertical partitioning	149

Table of Contents

Distributed caching   149
   Data-tier caching   149
      First-level caching   150
      Second-level caching   150
   Application-tier caching   150
      Memcached   150
      Redis   151
      Hazelcast   151
      Ehcache   151
      Riak   151
      Aerospike   152
      Infinispan   152
      Cache2k   152
   Other distributed caching   152
      Amazon ElastiCache   152
      Oracle distributed cache (Coherence)   152
Summary   153

Chapter 12: Microservice Basics   155

Monolithic architecture and its drawbacks   155
Introduction to microservices   156
   Independence and autonomy   157
   Resilience and fault tolerance   157
   Automated environment   157
   Stateless   158
Benefits of microservices   158
Microservice components   159
   Configuration server   159
   Load balancer   159
   Service discovery   160
   Circuit breaker   160
   Edge server   160
Microservice tools   160
   Netflix Eureka   161
   Netflix Zuul   161
   Spring Cloud Netflix   162
   Netflix Ribbon   162
   Netflix Hystrix   163
   Netflix Turbine   164
   HashiCorp Consul   164
   Eclipse MicroProfile   164

Table of Contents

Summary	165
Chapter 13: Ticket Management – Advanced CRUD	**167**
Ticket management using CRUD operations	167
Registration	168
User types	168
User POJO	168
Customer registration	170
Admin registration	172
CSR registration	174
Login and token management	175
Generating a token	175
Customer login	176
Admin login	177
CSR login	179
Ticket management	180
Ticket POJO	180
Getting a user by token	181
User Ticket management	182
Ticket controller	182
The UserTokenRequired interface	183
The UserTokenRequiredAspect class	184
Getting my tickets – customer	186
Allowing a user to view their single ticket	187
Allowing a customer to update a ticket	188
Updating a ticket – service (TicketServiceImpl)	188
Deleting a ticket	189
Deleting a service – service (TicketServiceImpl)	190
Deleting my ticket – API (ticket controller)	190
Admin Ticket management	191
Allowing a admin to view all tickets	191
Getting all tickets – service (TicketServiceImpl)	192
Getting all tickets – API (ticket controller)	192
The AdminTokenRequired interface	192
The AdminTokenRequiredAspect class	193
Admin updates a ticket	195
Updating a ticket by admin – service (TicketServiceImpl)	195
Allowing admin to view a single ticket	196
Allowing admin to delete tickets	196
Deleting tickets – service (TicketServiceImpl):	197
Deleting tickets by admin – API (ticket controller):	197
CSR Ticket management	198

CSR updates a ticket	198
CSRTokenRequired AOP	199
CSRTokenRequiredAspect	199
CSR view all tickets	201
Viewing all tickets by CSR – API (ticket controller)	201
CSR view single ticket	202
CSR delete tickets	202
Deleting tickets – service (TicketServivceImpl)	203
Deleting tickets by CSR – API (ticket controller)	203
Summary	**204**
Other Books You May Enjoy	**205**
Index	**209**

Preface

REST is an architectural style that tackles the challenges of building scalable web services. In today's connected world, APIs have taken a central role on the web. APIs provide the fabric through which systems interact, and REST has become synonymous with APIs. The depth, breadth, and ease of use of Spring makes it one of the most attractive frameworks in the Java ecosystem. Marrying the two technologies is, therefore, a very natural choice. Starting from the basics of the philosophy behind REST, this book goes through the necessary steps to design and implement an enterprise-grade RESTful web service. Taking a practical approach, each chapter provides code samples that you can apply to your own circumstances. This second edition brings forth the power of the latest Spring 5.0 release, working with built-in MVC, as well as the frontend framework. You'll learn techniques to deal with security in Spring and discover how to implement unit and integration test strategies.

Finally, the book ends by walking you through building a Java client for your RESTful web service, along with some scaling techniques using the new Spring Reactive libraries.

Who this book is for

This book is intended for those who want to learn to build RESTful web services with the latest Spring Framework 5.0. To make best use of the code samples included in the book, you should have a basic knowledge of the Java language. Previous experience with the Spring Framework will also help you get up and running quickly.

What this book covers

Chapter 1, *A Few Basics*, covers a basic understanding of REST, Reactive programming, and their basics, including the benefits of Reactive programming. It also covers Spring 5 basics with Reactive programming and an example RESTful web service as a base for other chapters.

Chapter 2, *Building RESTful Web Services in Spring 5 with Maven*, covers how to build a RESTful web service with Apache Maven by using either the Eclipse IDE or STS (Spring Tool Suite). The second section of the chapter covers creating a new project in Eclipse/STS and running our basic REST API.

Preface

Chapter 3, *Flux and Mono (Reactor Support) in Spring*, discusses Reactive programming and its benefits. This chapter also covers a little bit about Reactive Core and Reactive Streams. The second section of this chapter covers Flux and Mono in Spring REST, including a basic implementation of the `GET` and `POST` methods in Reactive.

Chapter 4, *CRUD Operations in Spring REST*, covers mapping CRUD operations to HTTP methods and implementation of CRUD operations on User with Reactor support.

Chapter 5, *CRUD Operations in Plain REST (Without Reactive) and File Upload*, covers mapping CRUD operations to HTTP methods and implementation of CRUD operations on User (Create, Read, Update, and Delete) without Reactor support. Also, this chapter covers file uploading in Spring.

Chapter 6, *Spring Security and JWT (JSON Web Token)*, covers Spring Security, JWT (JSON Web Token), and JWT generation. The second section of this chapter covers getting details from the generated token and also restricting service calls by JWT security.

Chapter 7, *Testing RESTful Web Services*, talks about various testing strategies to test our existing RESTful web services, including JUnit and MockMvc-like unit test cases, and clients such as Postman, SoapUI, and jsoup web reader.

Chapter 8, *Performance*, discusses different performance-related topics, including HTTP compression, HTTP caching, and HTTP control. The second section of the chapter covers cache implementation and HTTP headers such as `If-Modified-Since` and `ETag`.

Chapter 9, *AOP and Logger Controls*, covers Spring AOP, including its theory, implementation, and logging controls.

Chapter 10, *Building a REST Client and Error Handling*, covers `RestTemplate` in Spring, the basic setup for building a RESTful service client with Spring, and calling the RESTful service from the client side. The second section of the chapter covers error handling, including defining an error handler and using it.

Chapter 11, *Scaling*, covers the techniques, libraries, and tools used for application scaling purposes. It includes clustering and the benefits of clustering. This chapter also covers load balancing, scaling a database, and distributed caching.

Chapter 12, *Microservice Basics*, talks about microservices, the benefits of microservices, and the basic characteristics of microservices. It also covers various microservice components.

Chapter 13, *Ticket Management - Advanced CRUD*, covers advanced CRUD operations on tickets, including creating and updating a ticket through a customer, updating a ticket by CSR, and updating a ticket by admin. This chapter also talks about deleting multiple tickets by CSR and admin.

To get the most out of this book

The following is a descriptive list of the requirements to test all the code in this book:

- Hardware: 64-bit machine with minimum 2 GB RAM and min 5 GB of free hard disk space
- Software: Java 9, Maven 3.3.9, STS (Spring Tool Suite) 3.9.2
- Java 9: All code is tested on Java 9
- SoapUI: SoapUI 5.2.1 (free version) is used for REST API calls
- Postman: For REST client testing, Postman 5.0.4 is used

Download the example code files

You can download the example code files for this book from your account at `www.packtpub.com`. If you purchased this book elsewhere, you can visit `www.packtpub.com/support` and register to have the files emailed directly to you.

You can download the code files by following these steps:

1. Log in or register at `www.packtpub.com`.
2. Select the **SUPPORT** tab.
3. Click on **Code Downloads & Errata**.
4. Enter the name of the book in the **Search** box and follow the onscreen instructions.

Once the file is downloaded, please make sure that you unzip or extract the folder using the latest version of:

- WinRAR/7-Zip for Windows
- Zipeg/iZip/UnRarX for Mac
- 7-Zip/PeaZip for Linux

The code bundle for the book is also hosted on GitHub at https://github.com/PacktPublishing/Building-RESTful-Web-Services-with-Spring-5-Second-Edition. We also have other code bundles from our rich catalog of books and videos available at https://github.com/PacktPublishing/. Check them out!

Download the color images

We also provide a PDF file that has color images of the screenshots/diagrams used in this book. You can download it here: https://www.packtpub.com/sites/default/files/downloads/BuildingRESTfulWebServiceswithSpring5_ColorImages.pdf.

Conventions used

There are a number of text conventions used throughout this book.

CodeInText: Indicates code words in text, database table names, folder names, filenames, file extensions, pathnames, dummy URLs, user input, and Twitter handles. Here is an example: "Let's add a Logger to the class; in our case, we can use UserController."

A block of code is set as follows:

```
@ResponseBody
@RequestMapping("/test/aop/with/annotation")
@TokenRequired
public Map<String, Object> testAOPAnnotation(){
  Map<String, Object> map = new LinkedHashMap<>();
  map.put("result", "Aloha");
  return map;
}
```

When we wish to draw your attention to a particular part of a code block, the relevant lines or items are set in bold:

```
2018-01-15 16:29:55.951 INFO 17812 --- [nio-8080-exec-1]
com.packtpub.restapp.HomeController : {test} info
2018-01-15 16:29:55.951 WARN 17812 --- [nio-8080-exec-1]
com.packtpub.restapp.HomeController : {test} warn
2018-01-15 16:29:55.951 ERROR 17812 --- [nio-8080-exec-1]
com.packtpub.restapp.HomeController : {test} error
```

Any command-line input or output is written as follows:

```
mvn dependency:tree
```

Bold: Indicates a new term, an important word, or words that you see onscreen. For example, words in menus or dialog boxes appear in the text like this. Here is an example: "Now you can generate the project by clicking **Generate Project**."

Warnings or important notes appear like this.

Tips and tricks appear like this.

Get in touch

Feedback from our readers is always welcome.

General feedback: Email `feedback@packtpub.com` and mention the book title in the subject of your message. If you have questions about any aspect of this book, please email us at `questions@packtpub.com`.

Errata: Although we have taken every care to ensure the accuracy of our content, mistakes do happen. If you have found a mistake in this book, we would be grateful if you would report this to us. Please visit `www.packtpub.com/submit-errata`, selecting your book, clicking on the Errata Submission Form link, and entering the details.

Piracy: If you come across any illegal copies of our works in any form on the Internet, we would be grateful if you would provide us with the location address or website name. Please contact us at `copyright@packtpub.com` with a link to the material.

If you are interested in becoming an author: If there is a topic that you have expertise in and you are interested in either writing or contributing to a book, please visit `authors.packtpub.com`.

Reviews

Please leave a review. Once you have read and used this book, why not leave a review on the site that you purchased it from? Potential readers can then see and use your unbiased opinion to make purchase decisions, we at Packt can understand what you think about our products, and our authors can see your feedback on their book. Thank you!

For more information about Packt, please visit `packtpub.com`.

1
A Few Basics

As the world has moved into the big data era, collecting and dealing with data alone has become the main part of most of our web applications, and web services, too, as web services deal only with data, not the other parts of the user experience, look, and feel. Even though user experience is very important for all web applications, web services play a major role in dealing with data by consuming services from the client side.

In the early days of web services, **Simple Object Access Protocol** (**SOAP**) was the default choice for all backend developers who dealt with web service consumption. SOAP was mainly used in HTTP and **Simple Mail Transfer Protocol** (**SMTP**) for message transmission across the same or different platforms. When there was no **JavaScript Object Notation** (**JSON**) format available for web services, XML used to be the only available format SOAP could use for the web service consumption.

However, in the JSON era, **Representational State Transfer** (**REST**) started dominating web service based applications, as it supports multiple formats, including JSON, XML, and other formats. REST is simpler than SOAP, and the REST standards are easy to implement and consume. Also, REST is lightweight as compared to SOAP.

In this chapter, we will cover the following topics:

- REST—a basic understanding
- Reactive programming and its basics, including the benefits of Reactive programming
- Spring 5 basics with Reactive programming
- A sample RESTful web service that will be used as a base for the rest of the book

REST – a basic understanding

Contrary to popular belief, REST is not a protocol, but an architectural principle for managing state information. It's mainly used in web applications. REST was introduced by Roy Fielding to overcome implementation difficulties in SOAP. Roy's doctoral dissertation made for an easy way to retrieve data, regardless of the platform used. You will see all the components of RESTful web services in the following sections.

Uniform interface

In REST principles, all resources are identified by the **Uniform Resource Identifier (URI)**.

HTTP REST resources are represented in some media types, such as XML, JSON, and RDF. Also, RESTful resources are self-descriptive, which means enough information is given to describe how to process the request.

In another REST principle, the clients interact with servers through hypermedia, which is dynamically provided by the servers. Other than endpoints, clients don't need to know how to interact with RESTful services. This principle is referred to as **Hypermedia as the Engine of Application State (HATEOAS)**.

Client and server

By separating REST entities such as the client and server, we can reduce the complexity of REST principles, which will show clear boundaries between server and client. This decoupling will help developers concentrate on the client and server independently. Also, it will help to manage different roles for the client and server.

Stateless

In REST principles, the server will not keep any state about the client session on the server side; hence, it's stateless. If two calls are made to the server from a single client, the server will not identify whether both the calls are from the same client or not. As far as the server knows, every request is independent and new. Based on the URL, HTTP headers, and request body, including the parameters, the operation might be changed on the server side.

Cacheable

With RESTful web services, a client can cache any response coming from the server. The server can mention how, and for how long, it can cache the responses. With the caching option, a client can use the responses instead of contacting the server again. Also, caching will improve scalability and performance by avoiding client-server interactions all the time.

 This principle has significant advantages for scalability. Caching techniques will be discussed in Chapter 8, *Performance*.

Since REST typically leverages HTTP, it inherits all the caching properties that HTTP offers.

Layered system

By providing the layered system, a server can hide its identity. By doing this, clients won't know which server they are dealing with. This policy gives more security control by providing intermediate servers and supports the load-balancing feature, too. Also, intermediate servers can improve scalability and performance through load-balancing and shared caches.

Code on demand (COD)

Code on demand (COD) is considered an optional principle. Servers can extend the functionality of clients by transferring executable code. For example, JavaScript can be provided to web-based clients to customize the functionality. As code on demand reduces the visibility of the client side, this constraint is optional. Also not all APIs need this feature.

A Few Basics

More on REST

In web applications, REST is typically used over HTTP. REST doesn't need to be tied to any specific protocol. In HTTP REST, we mainly use the `GET`, `POST`, `PUT`, and `DELETE` methods to change the state of the resources we access. Other HTTP methods, such as `OPTIONS`, `HEAD`, `CONNECT`, and `TRACE`, can be used for more advanced operations, for example, for caching and debugging purposes. Most servers have disabled advanced methods for security and simplicity reasons; however, you can enable them by adjusting the server configuration files. As JSON is used as a primary media type for major applications, we also use only the JSON media type for our web service calls.

Imperative and Reactive programming

Let's see a small comparison between Imperative programming and Reactive programming: $x = y + z$.

In the preceding expression, assume $y = 10$ and $z = 15$. In this case, the x value would be 25. The value of x would be assigned at the time of the expression $x = y + z$. The value of x will never change after this expression.

This is perfectly alright in the traditional programming world. However, we might need a scenario where we should be able to follow up x when we change the value of y or z.

Our new scenario based values are:

- When $y = 20$ and $z = 15$, then $x = 35$
- When $y = 20$ and $z = 25$, then $x = 45$

The preceding scenario is not possible in Imperative programming, which we regularly use in our daily programming. But in some cases, we might need the value of x to be updated, corresponding to the change in y or z. Reactive programming is the perfect solution for this scenario. In Reactive programming, the value of x would automatically be updated, corresponding to the change in y or z.

Spreadsheet reference cells are the best example of Reactive programming. If a cell value changes, the referred cell value will be updated automatically. Another example can be found in a Model-View-Controller architecture, Reactive programming can automatically update the View, which is attached to the Model.

Reactive programming follows the Observer pattern to manipulate and transform the stream of data where the Publisher (observable) emits the items based on the Subscriber's need. As the Publisher emits the item, the Subscriber consumes those emitted items from the Publisher. Unlike the iterator pulling the items, here, the Publisher is pushing the items to the Subscriber.

As Reactive is a part of non-blocking architecture, it will be useful when we scale the application. Also, in non-blocking architecture, everything is considered as an event stream.

We will discuss more about Reactive in Java and Spring later in this chapter.

Reactive Streams

Reactive Streams are all about processing an asynchronous stream of data items, where applications react to data items as they receive them. This model is more memory-efficient, as it doesn't rely on any in-memory data.

Reactive Streams have four main components:

1. Publisher.
2. Subscriber.
3. Subscription.
4. Processor.

The Publisher publishes a stream of data, to which the Subscriber is asynchronously subscribed. The Processor transforms the data stream without the need for changing the Publisher or the Subscriber. The Processor (or multiple Processors) sits between the Publisher and the Subscriber to transform one stream of data to another.

Benefits of Reactive programming

The Reactive Streams approach is supported by engineers at Netflix, Pivotal, Twitter, Oracle, and TypeSafe. Especially, TypeSafe contributed more to Reactive Streams. Even Netflix engineers say, in their own words:

> *"Reactive programming with RxJava has enabled Netflix developers to leverage server-side concurrency without the typical thread-safety and synchronization concerns."*

A Few Basics

The following are the benefits of Reactive programming:

- Focuses on business logic
- Stream processing causes memory efficiency
- Overcomes low-level threading, synchronization, and concurrency issues

Reactive principles are used in real-time cases such as live database queries, big data, real-time analytics, HTTP/2, and so on.

Reactive programming in Java and Spring 5

RxJava was introduced by Netflix engineers to support the Reactive model in Java 8, with the bridge to Reactive Streams. However, Java started supporting the Reactive model with Java 9, and Reactive Streams have been incorporated into the JDK as `java.util.concurrent.Flow` in Java 9.

Also, Pivotal introduced the Reactor framework, which is built directly on Reactive Streams, avoiding the external bridge to Reactive Streams. A Reactor is considered as a 4th *generation* library.

Finally, Spring Framework 5.0 added Reactive features built into it, including the tools for HTTP servers and clients. Spring users find annotations and controllers handy when they deal with HTTP requests, especially dispatching Reactive requests and back pressure concerns to the framework.

The Reactive model seems to be efficient in resource utilization, as it can process higher loads with fewer threads. However, the Reactive model may not be the right solution for all problems. In some cases, Reactor may make things worse if we use it in the wrong section.

Our RESTful web service architecture

As we assume that our readers are familiar with Spring Framework, we will directly focus on the example service that we are going to build.

In this book, we are going to build a **Ticket Management System**. To give a clear picture of the Ticket Management System and how it's going to be used, we will come up with a scenario.

Let's assume that we have a banking web application used by our customers, Peter and Kevin, and we have Sammy, our admin, and Chloe, the **customer service representative** (**CSR**), to help in case of any banking application issues.

If Kevin/Peter is facing a problem in the web application, they can create a ticket in our Ticket Management System. This ticket will be handled by the admin and sent to CSR, who handles the ticket.

The CSR gets more information from the user and forwards the information to the technical team. Once the CSR resolves the issue, they can close the issue.

In our Ticket Management System we will be using the following components:

Ticket	• `ticketid` • `creatorid` • `createdat` • `content` • `severity` (minor, normal, major, critical) • `status` (open, in progress, resolved, reopened)
User	• `userid` • `username` • `usertype` (admin, general user, CSR)

In this Ticket Management System, we will focus on:

1. Creating a ticket by the user.
2. Updating the ticket by the user.
3. Updating the ticket status by the admin.
4. Updating the ticket status by the CSR.
5. Deleting the ticket by the user and admin.

In the initial chapters we will discuss User management to keep the business logic simple when we deal with topics such as AOP, Spring Security, and WebFlux. However, we will talk about the Ticket Management System in Chapter 13, *Ticket Management - Advanced CRUD* and implement all the business requirements that we mentioned earlier. In Chapter 13, *Ticket Management - Advanced CRUD* you will use all the advanced techniques employed in other chapters to finish our business requirements.

Summary

So far, we have gone through the basics of REST and Reactive programming and the necessity for Reactive Streams. We have gone through Spring 5 with Reactor support. Also, we have defined the business sample and architecture that will be used in the rest of the book.

In the next chapter, we will talk about simple project creation with Maven and the simple REST API. Also, we will discuss Maven file structure and dependencies, including samples.

2
Building RESTful Web Services in Spring 5 with Maven

In this chapter, we will build a simple REST web service that returns Aloha. Before moving to the implementation, we will focus on what components are involved in creating a RESTful web service. In this chapter, we will cover the following topics:

- Building a RESTful web service with Apache Maven
- Using the Eclipse IDE or STS for Spring REST project
- Creating a new project in Eclipse/STS
- Running and testing our REST API

Apache Maven

While building the Jakarta Turbine project, engineers found that managing the Ant build tool is hard. They needed a simple tool to build the projects with a clear definition that is easy to understand. Their attempt shaped Apache Maven, and the JARs can be shared across several projects in the central place.

 More information on Maven can be found at https://maven.apache.org.

Apache Maven was created to support Java project and build management. Also, its simplified definition makes Java developers' lives easy while building and deploying Java projects.

At the time of writing this book, Apache Maven's latest version is 3.5.0, and it can be downloaded from their website: https://maven.apache.org/download.cgi.

 Maven 3.3+ requires JDK 1.7 or above. So please make sure of your Java version when you use Maven 3.3.

You can get the binary or source ZIP files (or whatever the desired format for your operating system is) from the preceding link and install Maven on to your computer.

Maven installation can be verified by entering the `mvn --version` command in your console/command prompt. If it is installed successfully, it will show the following details (only on a Windows operating system):

```
Administrator: Command Prompt

C:\>mvn --version
C:\
Apache Maven 3.3.9 (bb52d8502b132ec0a5a3f4c09453c07478323dc5; 2015-11-10T11:41:47-05:00)
Maven home: C:\apache-maven-3.3.9\bin\..
Java version: 1.8.0_91, vendor: Oracle Corporation
Java home: C:\Program Files\Java\jdk1.8.0_91\jre
Default locale: en_CA, platform encoding: Cp1252
OS name: "windows 10", version: "10.0", arch: "amd64", family: "dos"

C:\>
```

For clarity, the following image shows a Maven version check performed on Ubuntu:

```
Apache Maven 3.0.5
Maven home: /usr/share/maven
Java version: 1.8.0_121, vendor: Oracle Corporation
Java home: /usr/lib/jvm/java-8-oracle/jre
Default locale: en_US, platform encoding: UTF-8
OS name: "linux", version: "3.13.0-105-generic", arch: "amd64", family: "unix"
```

Creating a project with Maven

Once Maven is installed and verified, you will have to create a project with Maven. This you can do in the command prompt itself. Just run the following command in your desired location, then the project will be created automatically:

```
mvn archetype:generate -DgroupId=com.packtpub.restapp -DartifactId=ticket-management -DarchetypeArtifactId=maven-archetype-quickstart -DinteractiveMode=false -Dversion=1.0.0-SNAPSHOT
```

If you face any problems while creating the project, use the –X option in Maven, shown as follows. It will point out the location where the error has occurred:

```
mvn -X archetype:generate -DgroupId=com.packtpub.restapp -DartifactId=ticket-management -DarchetypeArtifactId=maven-archetype-quickstart -DinteractiveMode=false -Dversion=1.0.0-SNAPSHOT
```

In the following points, we go through each part of the command that is used to create a Maven project:

- `archetype:generate`: Use this if the goal is to create a new project on a specified archetype, in our case `maven-archetype-quickstart`.
- `-Dgroupid=com.packtpub.restapp`: This part defines a project with a group identifier such as a package.
- `-DartifcatId=ticket-management`: This part defines our project name (folder).
- `-DarchetypeArtifactId=maven-archetype-quickstart`: This part will be used to select the archetype on the `archetype:generate` goal.
- `-Dversion=1.0.0-SNAPSHOT`: The project version can be mentioned in this part. It will be helpful when you deploy the project and distribute it.

Viewing a POM file after creating a project

Once we have created a project, we can see the `pom.xml` file in our project folder. It will have all the basic details, such as `groupId`, `name`, and so on. Also, you can see the default `Junit` dependency under the `dependencies` configuration part:

```
<project xmlns="http://maven.apache.org/POM/4.0.0"
xmlns:xsi="http://www.w3.org/2001/XMLSchema-instance"
xsi:schemaLocation="http://maven.apache.org/POM/4.0.0
http://maven.apache.org/maven-v4_0_0.xsd">
  <modelVersion>4.0.0</modelVersion>
```

```xml
<groupId>com.packtpub.restapp</groupId>
<artifactId>ticket-management</artifactId>
<packaging>jar</packaging>
<version>1.0-SNAPSHOT</version>
<name>ticket-management</name>
<url>http://maven.apache.org</url>
<dependencies>
  <dependency>
    <groupId>junit</groupId>
    <artifactId>junit</artifactId>
    <version>3.8.1</version>
    <scope>test</scope>
  </dependency>
</dependencies>
</project>
```

Maven artifacts belong to a group (typically `com.organization.product`), and must have a unique identifier. In the preceding POM file, the SNAPSHOT suffix in version tells Maven that this project is still in development.

POM file structure

Here we will check the **Project Object Model (POM)** file structure, looking into how it's organized and what parts are available inside the pom.xml file. The POM file can have properties, dependencies, build, and profiles. However, these parts will vary for different projects. We might not need some of them in other projects:

```xml
<project>
  // basic project info comes here
  <properties>
    // local project based properties can be stored here
  <properties>
  <dependencies>
    // all third party dependencies come here
  </dependencies>
  <build>
    <plugins>
      // build plugin and compiler arguments come here
    </plugins>
  </build>
  <profiles>
    All profiles like staging, production come here
  </profiles>
```

Chapter 2

```
</project>
```

Understanding POM dependencies

Maven helps manage the third-party libraries in your operating system. In the olden days, you might have had to copy each third-party library into your project manually. This could be a big problem when you had more than one project. Maven avoids this third-party libraries management confusion by keeping all libraries in a central place for each operating system. Regardless of your project count, the third-party libraries will be downloaded to the system only once.

Maven repositories can be found at `https://mvnrepository.com/`.

Every operating system has their own local Maven repository location:

- Windows Maven central repository location: `C:\Users\<username>\.m2\repository\`
- Linux Maven central repository location: `/home/<username>/.m2/repository`
- MAC Maven central repository location: `/Users/<username>/.m2/repository`

Whenever you add a third-party library to your POM dependency, the specified JAR and related files will be copied into the location `\.m2\repository`.

We will learn about the Maven dependency structure by looking at one sample. Let's assume that we need to use Log4j version 2.9.1 in our application. In order to use it, we need to add the dependency to our project. We can search the `log4j-core` dependency from `https://mvnrepository.com` and copy the dependency into our POM under `dependencies`.

[19]

A sample Maven dependency is as follows:

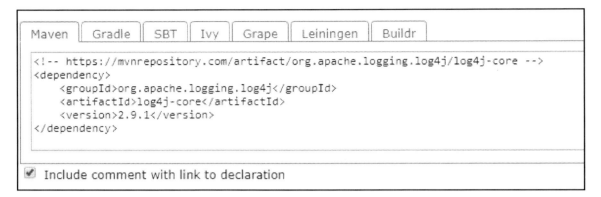

Adding Log4j 2.9.1 to POM dependency

Once the dependency is added and the project is updated on your IDE, the corresponding library will be copied into `\.m2\repository`:

```
<dependency>
    <groupId>org.apache.logging.log4j</groupId>
    <artifactId>log4j-core</artifactId>
    <version>2.9.1</version>
</dependency>
```

The preceding dependency, `log4j-core`, will be added under POM. In this dependency, you can see `groupId`, `artifactId`, and `version` explained as follows:

- `groupId` is used to make the JAR/WAR file unique across all projects. As it will be used globally, Maven recommends that the package names follow the same rules as that of domain names with subgroups. A sample `groupId` is `com.google.appengine`. However, some third-party dependencies don't follow the `groupId` package-naming policy. Check the following sample:

    ```
    <dependency>
        <groupId>joda-time</groupId>
        <artifactId>joda-time</artifactId>
        <version>2.9.9</version>
    </dependency>
    ```

- `artifactId` is just the name of the JAR/WAR file without the extension.
- `version` comes with number to show the JAR file version. Some JAR files come with extra information, such as `RELEASE`, for example, `3.1.4.RELEASE`. The following code will download the `spring-security-web` library `3.1.4` JAR file to the repository location:

```
<dependency>
    <groupId>org.springframework.security</groupId>
    <artifactId>spring-security-web</artifactId>
    <version>3.1.4.RELEASE</version>
</dependency>
```

The `Log4j-core` files (in Windows) will appear as follows:

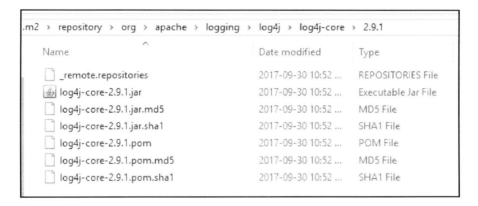

Sometimes, you may see the `.jar` file missing when you update the project on IDE. In such cases, delete the whole folder (in our case `log4j-core` folder) and update them once again. In order to update the missing JAR file, after you delete the folder, just update your IDE (STS /Eclipse in our case) by right clicking the project and select **Maven | Update Project**. Finally, make sure you have the `.jar` file available under the folder.

[21]

Sample repositories in `.m2\repository` should appear as follows:

When you update a project (in Eclipse or any other IDE), it will get the JAR and related files from a remote Maven repository to your system's central repository.

Dependency trees

Dependency trees can be used in projects to locate specific dependencies. If you are wondering about any specific libraries, such as why it's used, you can check by executing a dependency tree. Also, a dependency tree can be expanded to display dependency conflicts.

The following code shows the dependency libraries and how they're organized:

```
mvn dependency:tree
```

By executing the command on your project folder (or wherever the pom.xml file is available), you can view the dependency tree, and its structure is as follows:

```
[INFO] --- maven-dependency-plugin:2.8:tree (default-cli) @ ticket-management ---
[INFO] com.packtpub.restapp:ticket-management:jar:0.0.1-SNAPSHOT
[INFO] +- org.springframework:spring-web:jar:5.0.0.RELEASE:compile
[INFO] |  +- org.springframework:spring-beans:jar:5.0.0.RELEASE:compile
[INFO] |  \- org.springframework:spring-core:jar:5.0.0.RELEASE:compile
[INFO] |     \- org.springframework:spring-jcl:jar:5.0.0.RELEASE:compile
[INFO] +- org.springframework.boot:spring-boot-starter-tomcat:jar:1.5.7.RELEASE:compile
[INFO] |  +- org.apache.tomcat.embed:tomcat-embed-core:jar:8.5.20:compile
[INFO] |  +- org.apache.tomcat.embed:tomcat-embed-el:jar:8.5.20:compile
[INFO] |  \- org.apache.tomcat.embed:tomcat-embed-websocket:jar:8.5.20:compile
[INFO] +- org.springframework.boot:spring-boot-starter:jar:1.5.7.RELEASE:compile
[INFO] |  +- org.springframework.boot:spring-boot:jar:1.5.7.RELEASE:compile
[INFO] |  +- org.springframework.boot:spring-boot-autoconfigure:jar:1.5.7.RELEASE:compile
[INFO] |  +- org.springframework.boot:spring-boot-starter-logging:jar:1.5.7.RELEASE:compile
[INFO] |  |  +- ch.qos.logback:logback-classic:jar:1.1.11:compile
[INFO] |  |  |  \- ch.qos.logback:logback-core:jar:1.1.11:compile
[INFO] |  |  +- org.slf4j:jcl-over-slf4j:jar:1.7.25:compile
[INFO] |  |  +- org.slf4j:jul-to-slf4j:jar:1.7.25:compile
[INFO] |  |  \- org.slf4j:log4j-over-slf4j:jar:1.7.25:compile
[INFO] |  \- org.yaml:snakeyaml:jar:1.17:runtime
[INFO] +- com.fasterxml.jackson.core:jackson-databind:jar:2.9.2:compile
[INFO] |  +- com.fasterxml.jackson.core:jackson-annotations:jar:2.9.0:compile
[INFO] |  \- com.fasterxml.jackson.core:jackson-core:jar:2.9.2:compile
[INFO] +- org.springframework:spring-webmvc:jar:5.0.1.RELEASE:compile
[INFO] |  +- org.springframework:spring-aop:jar:5.0.1.RELEASE:compile
[INFO] |  +- org.springframework:spring-context:jar:5.0.1.RELEASE:compile
[INFO] |  \- org.springframework:spring-expression:jar:5.0.1.RELEASE:compile
[INFO] +- org.springframework.boot:spring-boot-starter-test:jar:1.5.7.RELEASE:test
[INFO] |  +- org.springframework.boot:spring-boot-test:jar:1.5.7.RELEASE:test
[INFO] |  +- org.springframework.boot:spring-boot-test-autoconfigure:jar:1.5.7.RELEASE:test
[INFO] |  +- com.jayway.jsonpath:json-path:jar:2.2.0:test
[INFO] |  |  +- net.minidev:json-smart:jar:2.2.1:test
[INFO] |  |  |  \- net.minidev:accessors-smart:jar:1.1:test
[INFO] |  |  |     \- org.ow2.asm:asm:jar:5.0.3:test
```

```
[INFO] |  |  \- org.slf4j:slf4j-api:jar:1.7.16:compile
[INFO] |  +- junit:junit:jar:4.12:test
[INFO] |  +- org.assertj:assertj-core:jar:2.6.0:test
[INFO] |  +- org.mockito:mockito-core:jar:1.10.19:test
[INFO] |  |  \- org.objenesis:objenesis:jar:2.1:test
[INFO] |  +- org.hamcrest:hamcrest-core:jar:1.3:test
[INFO] |  +- org.hamcrest:hamcrest-library:jar:1.3:test
[INFO] |  +- org.skyscreamer:jsonassert:jar:1.4.0:test
[INFO] |  |  \- com.vaadin.external.google:android-json:jar:0.0.20131108.vaadin1:test
[INFO] |  \- org.springframework:spring-test:jar:4.3.11.RELEASE:test
[INFO] +- io.jsonwebtoken:jjwt:jar:0.6.0:compile
[INFO] \- org.springframework.boot:spring-boot-starter-aop:jar:1.5.7.RELEASE:compile
[INFO] \- org.aspectj:aspectjweaver:jar:1.8.10:compile
```

Spring Boot

Spring Boot is a quick and easily configurable Spring application. Unlike other Spring applications, we don't need much configuration to build a Spring Boot application, so you can start building it very quickly and easily.

Spring Boot helps us to create a standalone application, which can be embedded with Tomcat or another container quickly.

Developing RESTful web services

To create a new project, we can use a Maven command prompt or an online tool, such as Spring Initializr (http://start.spring.io), to generate the project base. This website comes in handy for creating a simple Spring Boot-based web project to start the ball rolling.

Creating a project base

Let's go to http://start.spring.io in our browser and configure our project by filling in the following parameters to create a project base:

- **Group**: com.packtpub.restapp
- **Artifact**: ticket-management
- **Search for dependencies**: Web (full-stack web development with Tomcat and Spring MVC)

Chapter 2

After configuring our project, it will look as shown in the following screenshot:

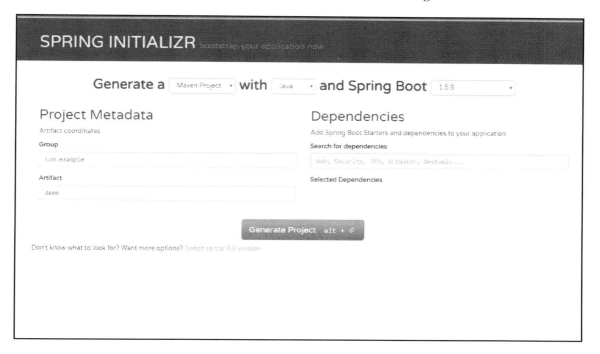

Now you can generate the project by clicking **Generate Project**. The project (ZIP file) should be downloaded to your system. Unzip the `.zip` file and you should see the files as shown in the following screenshot:

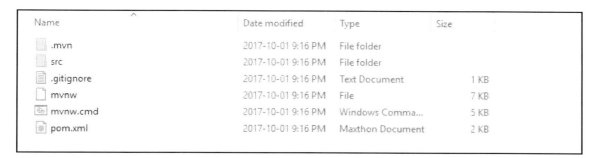

Copy the entire folder (`ticket-management`) and keep it in your desired location.

Building RESTful Web Services in Spring 5 with Maven

Working with your favorite IDE

Now is the time to pick the IDE. Though there are many IDEs used for Spring Boot projects, I would recommend using **Spring Tool Suite** (**STS**), as it is open source and easy to manage projects with. In my case, I use `sts-3.8.2.RELEASE`. You can download the latest STS from this link: `https://spring.io/tools/sts/all`. In most cases, you may not need to install; just unzip the file and start using it:

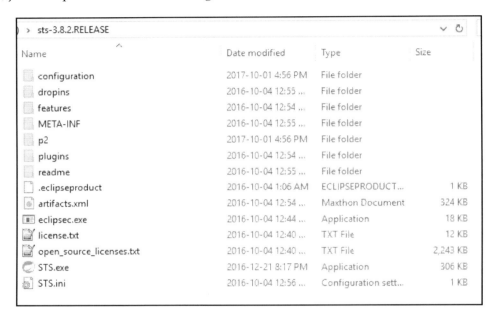

After extracting the STS, you can start using the tool by running `STS.exe` (shown in the preceding screenshot).

In STS, you can import the project by selecting **Existing Maven Projects**, shown as follows:

Chapter 2

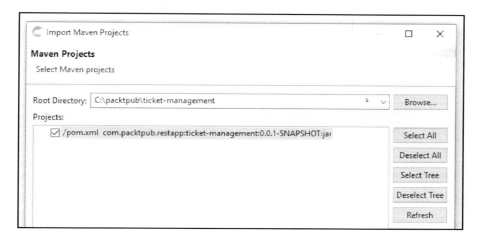

After importing the project, you can see the project in **Package Explorer**, as shown in the following screenshot:

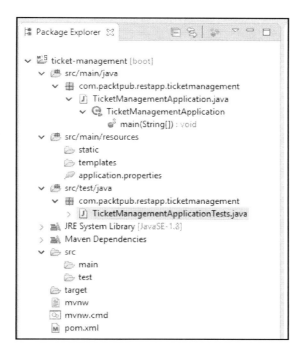

You can see the main Java file (`TicketManagementApplication`) by default:

```java
TicketManagementApplication.java
    package com.packtpub.restapp.ticketmanagement;

    import org.springframework.boot.SpringApplication;
    import org.springframework.boot.autoconfigure.SpringBootApplication;

    @SpringBootApplication
    public class TicketManagementApplication {

        public static void main(String[] args) {
            SpringApplication.run(TicketManagementApplication.class, args);
        }
    }
```

To simplify the project, we will clean up the existing POM file and update the required dependencies. Add this file configuration to `pom.xml`:

```xml
<?xml version="1.0" encoding="UTF-8"?>
<project xmlns="http://maven.apache.org/POM/4.0.0"
xmlns:xsi="http://www.w3.org/2001/XMLSchema-instance"
  xsi:schemaLocation="http://maven.apache.org/POM/4.0.0
http://maven.apache.org/xsd/maven-4.0.0.xsd">
    <modelVersion>4.0.0</modelVersion>
    <groupId>com.packtpub.restapp</groupId>
    <artifactId>ticket-management</artifactId>
    <version>0.0.1-SNAPSHOT</version>
    <packaging>jar</packaging>
    <name>ticket-management</name>
    <description>Demo project for Spring Boot</description>
    <properties>
        <project.build.sourceEncoding>UTF-8</project.build.sourceEncoding>
<project.reporting.outputEncoding>UTF-8</project.reporting.outputEncoding>
    </properties>
    <dependencies>
        <dependency>
        <groupId>org.springframework</groupId>
        <artifactId>spring-web</artifactId>
        <version>5.0.1.RELEASE</version>
        </dependency>
        <dependency>
            <groupId>org.springframework.boot</groupId>
            <artifactId>spring-boot-starter</artifactId>
            <version>1.5.7.RELEASE</version>
        </dependency>
        <dependency>
            <groupId>org.springframework.boot</groupId>
```

```xml
            <artifactId>spring-boot-starter-tomcat</artifactId>
            <version>1.5.7.RELEASE</version>
        </dependency>
        <dependency>
            <groupId>com.fasterxml.jackson.core</groupId>
            <artifactId>jackson-databind</artifactId>
            <version>2.9.2</version>
        </dependency>
        <dependency>
            <groupId>org.springframework</groupId>
            <artifactId>spring-web</artifactId>
            <version>5.0.0.RELEASE</version>
        </dependency>
        <dependency>
            <groupId>org.springframework</groupId>
            <artifactId>spring-webmvc</artifactId>
            <version>5.0.1.RELEASE</version>
        </dependency>
        <dependency>
            <groupId>org.springframework.boot</groupId>
            <artifactId>spring-boot-starter-test</artifactId>
            <scope>test</scope>
            <version>1.5.7.RELEASE</version>
        </dependency>
    </dependencies>
    <build>
        <plugins>
            <plugin>
                <groupId>org.springframework.boot</groupId>
                <artifactId>spring-boot-maven-plugin</artifactId>
            </plugin>
        </plugins>
    </build>
</project>
```

In the preceding configuration, you can check that we have used the following libraries:

- `spring-web`
- `spring-boot-starter`
- `spring-boot-starter-tomcat`
- `spring-bind`
- `jackson-databind`

As the preceding dependencies are needed for the project to run, we have added them to our `pom.xml` file.

So far we have got the base project ready for Spring Web Service. Let's add a basic REST code to the application. First, remove the `@SpringBootApplication` annotation from the `TicketManagementApplication` class and add the following annotations:

```
@Configuration
@EnableAutoConfiguration
@ComponentScan
@Controller
```

These annotations will help the class to act as a web service class. I am not going to talk much about what these configurations will do in this chapter. After adding the annotations, please add a simple method to return a string as our basic web service method:

```
@ResponseBody
@RequestMapping("/")
public String sayAloha(){
   return "Aloha";
}
```

Finally, your code will look as follows:

```
package com.packtpub.restapp.ticketmanagement;
import org.springframework.boot.SpringApplication;
import org.springframework.boot.autoconfigure.EnableAutoConfiguration;
import org.springframework.context.annotation.ComponentScan;
import org.springframework.context.annotation.Configuration;
import org.springframework.stereotype.Controller;
import org.springframework.web.bind.annotation.RequestMapping;
import org.springframework.web.bind.annotation.ResponseBody;
@Configuration
@EnableAutoConfiguration
@ComponentScan
@Controller
public class TicketManagementApplication {
```

```
@ResponseBody
@RequestMapping("/")
public String sayAloha(){
  return "Aloha";
}
public static void main(String[] args) {
  SpringApplication.run(TicketManagementApplication.class, args);
}
}
```

Once all the coding changes are done, just run the project on Spring Boot App (**Run As** | **Spring Boot App**). You can verify the application has loaded by checking this message in the console:

`Tomcat started on port(s): 8080 (http)`

Once verified, you can check the API on the browser by simply typing `localhost:8080`. Check out the following screenshot:

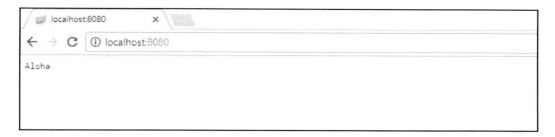

If you want to change the port number, you can configure a different port number in `application.properties`, **which is in** `src/main/resources/application.properties`. Check out the following screenshot:

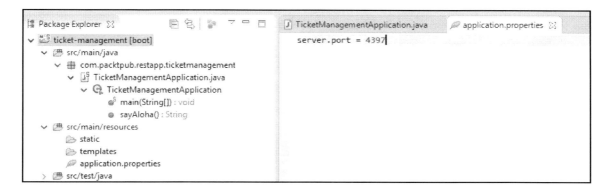

[31]

Summary

In this chapter, we have seen how to set up a Maven build to support the basic implementation of a web service. Also, we have learned how Maven is helpful in third-party library management as well as Spring Boot and basic Spring REST projects. In the coming chapters, we will discuss more about Spring REST endpoints and Reactor support.

3
Flux and Mono (Reactor Support) in Spring

In this chapter, we will walk the reader through more practical approaches to supporting Reactor in Spring 5, including Flux and Mono. The user will get hands-on experience with Flux and Mono, with simple JSON as the result.

We will cover the following topics in this chapter:

- Reactive programming and benefits
- Reactive Core and Streams
- Flux and Mono in Spring REST
- User classes with Reactive—REST

Benefits of Reactive programming

Let's assume we have one million user transactions happening in our application. Next year, it is going to increase to 10 million, so we need to scale it. The traditional method of doing this is to add enough servers (horizontal scaling).

Instead of doing horizontal scaling, what if we get an option to scale with the same servers? Yes, Reactive programming will help us to do that. Reactive programming is all about non-blocking applications that are synchronous and event-driven, and it doesn't require a lot of threads to scale vertically (within the JVM) rather than horizontally (through clustering).

Reactive types are not intended to process requests faster. However, they focus more on request concurrency, especially requesting data from a remote server efficiently. With Reactive type support, you will get higher-quality service. While comparing traditional processing, which blocks the current thread while waiting for a result, a Reactive API requests only the amount of data that can be consumed. Reactive APIs deal with streams of data, not only with individual elements one by one.

Overall, Reactive programming is about non-blocking, event-driven applications that can be scaled with a small number of threads, with back pressure as a main component to make sure the producers (emitters) do not overwhelm consumers (receivers).

Reactive Core and Streams

Java 8 introduced Reactive Core, which implements the Reactive programming model and is built on top of the Reactive Streams specification, a standard for building Reactive applications. As the lambda syntax gives more flexibility to go for the event-driven approach Java 8 provides the best way to support Reactive. Also, Java's lambda syntax gives us the ability to create and spawn up small and independent asynchronous tasks. One of the main goals of Reactive Streams is to address the problem of back pressure. We will talk more about back pressure in a later section of this chapter.

The main difference between Java 8 Streams and Reactive Streams is that Reactive is a push model, whereas Java 8 Streams focuses on pulling. In Reactive Streams, based on consumer needs and numbers, all events will be pushed to consumers.

Reactive programming model support is Spring 5's best feature since the last release. Also, with the support of the Akka and Play framework, Java 8 provides a better platform for Reactive applications.

Reactor is built on top of the Reactive Streams specification. Reactive Streams is a bundle of four Java interfaces:

- `Publisher`
- `Subscriber`
- `Subscription`
- `Processor`

`Publisher` will publish a stream of data items to the subscribers that registered with the `Publisher`. Using an executor, the `Publisher` publishes the items to the `Subscriber`. Also, `Publisher` makes sure that the `Subscriber` method invocations for each subscription are strictly ordered.

`Subscriber` consumes items only when requested. You can cancel the receiving process any time by using `Subscription`.

`Subscription` behaves as a message mediator between the `Publisher` and the `Subscriber`.

`Processor` represents a processing stage, which can include both `Subscriber` and a `Publisher`. `Processor` can initiate back pressure and cancel the subscription, as well.

Reactive Streams is a specification for asynchronous stream processing, which means all events can be produced and consumed asynchronously.

Back pressures and Reactive Streams

Back pressure is a mechanism that authorizes the receiver to define how much data it wants from the emitter (data provider). The main objective of Reactive Streams is all about handling back pressure. It allows:

- The control to go to the receiver, to get data after it is ready to be processed
- Defining and controlling the amount of data to be received
- Efficient handling of the slow emitter / fast receiver or fast emitter / slow receiver scenarios

WebFlux

As of September 2017, Spring announced the general availability of 5. Spring 5 introduced a Reactive web framework called Spring WebFlux. It is a non-blocking web framework that uses Reactor to support the Reactive Streams API.

As traditionally, blocking threads consume resources, there was a necessity for non-blocking async programming to play a better role. The Spring tech team introduced a non-blocking async programming model to handle a large number of concurrent requests, especially for latency-sensitive workloads. This concept will be mainly used in mobile applications and microservices. Also, this WebFlux will be the best fix for scenarios with many clients and uneven workloads.

Basic REST API

To understand the practical part of Reactive components such as Flux and Mono, we will have to create our own REST API and start implementing Flux and Mono classes in our API. In this chapter, we will build a simple REST web service that returns `Aloha`. Before moving into the implementation part, we will focus on the components involved in creating a RESTful web service.

In this section, we will cover the following topics:

- Flux and Mono—introduction of Spring 5: Functional Web Framework components
- Flux and Mono—in the REST API

Flux

Flux is one of the main types in Reactor. A Flux is the equivalent of an RxJava Observable, capable of emitting zero or more items, and then, optionally, either completing or failing.

Flux is one of the Reactive types that implement the `Publisher` interface from the Reactive Streams manifesto. Flux's main role is to deal with streams of data. Flux mainly represents a stream of *N* elements.

Flux is a publisher, a sequence of events of a specific **Plain Old Java Object (POJO)** type.

Mono

Mono is another type of Reactor can emit only one item at the most. An asynchronous task that just wants to signal completion can use a Mono. Mono mainly deals with a stream of one element, as opposed to Flux's *N* elements.

Both Flux and Mono make use of this semantic by coercing to the relevant type when using some operations. For example, concatenating two Monos together will produce a Flux; on the other hand, calling `single()` on `Flux<T>` will return a `Mono <T>`.

Both Flux and Mono are **Reactive Streams** (**RS**) publisher implementations and conform to Reactive-pull back pressure.

Mono is used in specific scenarios like an HTTP request that produces only one response. In such cases, using Mono would be the right choice.

Returning a `Mono<HttpResponse>` for an HTTP request like the scenario mentioned earlier is better than returning a `Flux<HttpResponse>`, as it offers only operators that are relevant to a context of zero items or one item.

Mono can be used to represent no-value asynchronous processes that only have the concept of completion.

User class with Reactive – REST

In the first chapter, we introduced `Ticket` and `User`, two classes involved with our web service. As the `Ticket` class is a little complex compared to the `User` class, we will use the `User` class to understand Reactive components.

As Reactive in Spring 5 is not fully stable yet, we are going to talk about Reactive in only a few chapters. So we will create a separate package for Reactive-based REST APIs. Also, we will add Reactive-based dependencies in our existing `pom.xml` file.

First, we will have to add all Reactive dependencies. Here, we will add the code in our existing `pom.xml` file:

```xml
<?xml version="1.0" encoding="UTF-8"?>
<project xmlns="http://maven.apache.org/POM/4.0.0"
xmlns:xsi="http://www.w3.org/2001/XMLSchema-instance"
  xsi:schemaLocation="http://maven.apache.org/POM/4.0.0
http://maven.apache.org/xsd/maven-4.0.0.xsd">
   <modelVersion>4.0.0</modelVersion>
   <groupId>com.packtpub.restapp</groupId>
   <artifactId>ticket-management</artifactId>
   <version>0.0.1-SNAPSHOT</version>
   <packaging>jar</packaging>
   <name>ticket-management</name>
   <description>Demo project for Spring Boot</description>
<properties>
    <project.build.sourceEncoding>UTF-8</project.build.sourceEncoding>
<project.reporting.outputEncoding>UTF-8</project.reporting.outputEncoding>
</properties>
<dependencyManagement>
   <dependencies>
    <dependency>
      <groupId>io.projectreactor</groupId>
      <artifactId>reactor-bom</artifactId>
      <version>Bismuth-RELEASE</version>
         <type>pom</type>
         <scope>import</scope>
    </dependency>
      </dependencies>
</dependencyManagement>
<dependencies>
    <dependency>
    <groupId>org.springframework</groupId>
    <artifactId>spring-web</artifactId>
    <version>5.0.1.RELEASE</version>
   </dependency>
   <dependency>
    <groupId>org.springframework.boot</groupId>
    <artifactId>spring-boot-starter</artifactId>
    <version>1.5.7.RELEASE</version>
   </dependency>
   <dependency>
    <groupId>org.springframework.boot</groupId>
    <artifactId>spring-boot-starter-tomcat</artifactId>
    <version>1.5.7.RELEASE</version>
   </dependency>
   <dependency>
```

```xml
      <groupId>com.fasterxml.jackson.core</groupId>
      <artifactId>jackson-databind</artifactId>
      <version>2.9.2</version>
   </dependency>
   <dependency>
      <groupId>org.springframework</groupId>
      <artifactId>spring-web</artifactId>
      <version>5.0.0.RELEASE</version>
   </dependency>
   <dependency>
      <groupId>org.springframework</groupId>
      <artifactId>spring-webmvc</artifactId>
      <version>5.0.1.RELEASE</version>
   </dependency>
   <dependency>
      <groupId>org.springframework.boot</groupId>
      <artifactId>spring-boot-starter-test</artifactId>
      <scope>test</scope>
      <version>1.5.7.RELEASE</version>
   </dependency>
   <dependency>
      <groupId>org.reactivestreams</groupId>
      <artifactId>reactive-streams</artifactId>
   </dependency>
   <dependency>
      <groupId>io.projectreactor</groupId>
      <artifactId>reactor-core</artifactId>
   </dependency>
   <dependency>
      <groupId>io.projectreactor.ipc</groupId>
      <artifactId>reactor-netty</artifactId>
   </dependency>
   <dependency>
      <groupId>org.apache.tomcat.embed</groupId>
      <artifactId>tomcat-embed-core</artifactId>
      <version>8.5.4</version>
   </dependency>
   <dependency>
      <groupId>org.springframework</groupId>
      <artifactId>spring-context</artifactId>
      <version>5.0.0.RELEASE</version>
   </dependency>
   <dependency>
      <groupId>org.springframework</groupId>
      <artifactId>spring-webflux</artifactId>
      <version>5.0.0.RELEASE</version>
   </dependency>
</dependencies>
```

Flux and Mono (Reactor Support) in Spring

```xml
<build>
  <plugins>
    <plugin>
      <groupId>org.springframework.boot</groupId>
      <artifactId>spring-boot-maven-plugin</artifactId>
    </plugin>
  </plugins>
</build>
</project>
```

For Reactive-related work, you can either use an existing project, or you can create a new project to avoid conflicts with the Non-Reactive (plain) REST API. You can use https://start.spring.io to get the basic project, and then update the Maven file with the preceding configuration.

In the preceding POM configuration, we have added Reactor dependencies on top of our existing dependencies (mentioned as follows):

- reactive-streams
- reactor-core
- reactor-netty
- tomcat-embed-core
- spring-webflux

These are the libraries needed in order to work with Reactors.

The User class components are as follows:

- userid
- username
- user_email
- user_type (admin, general user, CSR)

Here, we have four variables used for the User class. To make it simpler to understand Reactive components, we use only two variables (userid, username). Let's create a POJO class with only userid and username.

The `User` POJO class is as follows:

```
package com.packtpub.reactive;
public class User {
  private Integer userid;
  private String username;
  public User(Integer userid, String username){
    this.userid = userid;
    this.username = username;
  }
  public Integer getUserid() {
    return userid;
  }
  public void setUserid(Integer userid) {
    this.userid = userid;
  }
  public String getUsername() {
    return username;
  }
  public void setUsername(String username) {
    this.username = username;
  }
}
```

In the preceding class, I have used two variables and a constructor to fill the variables while instantiating. Also, getters/setters are used to access those variables.

Let's create a Reactive repository for the `User` class:

```
package com.packtpub.reactive;
import reactor.core.publisher.Flux;
public interface UserRepository {
  Flux<User> getAllUsers();
}
```

In the preceding code, we have introduced a Reactive repository for `User` and a class with only one method, called `getAllUsers`. By using this method, we should be able to retrieve a list of users. Let's not talk about Flux now, as it will be discussed later.

You can see that this `UserRepository` is an interface. We need to have a concrete class to implement this interface in order to use this repository. Let's create a concrete class for this Reactive repository:

```
package com.packtpub.reactive;
import java.util.HashMap;
import java.util.Map;
import reactor.core.publisher.Flux;
```

```
public class UserRepositorySample implements UserRepository {
  // initiate Users
  private Map<Integer, User> users = null;
  // fill dummy values for testing
  public UserRepositorySample() {
    // Java 9 Immutable map used
    users = Map.of(
      1, (new User(1, "David")),
      2, (new User(2, "John")),
      3, (new User(3, "Kevin"))
    );
  }
  // this method will return all users
  @Override
  public Flux<User> getAllUsers() {
    return Flux.fromIterable(this.users.values());
  }
}
```

As Java 9 has immutable map available, we can make use of Immutable maps in our code. However these immutable objects applicable only for this chapter as we don't do any update on the existing entries.

In next chapter, we will use regular map as we need to edit them in CRUD operations.

At the moment, we are able to get a list of users from the concrete class. Right now we need a web handler to retrieve the users in the controller. Let's create a handler now:

```
package com.packtpub.reactive;
import org.springframework.web.reactive.function.server.ServerRequest;
import org.springframework.web.reactive.function.server.ServerResponse;
import static org.springframework.http.MediaType.APPLICATION_JSON;
import reactor.core.publisher.Flux;
import reactor.core.publisher.Mono;
public class UserHandler {
  private final UserRepository userRepository;
  public UserHandler(UserRepository userRepository){
    this.userRepository = userRepository;
  }
  public Mono<ServerResponse> getAllUsers(ServerRequest request){
    Flux<User> users = this.userRepository.getAllUsers();
    return ServerResponse.ok().contentType(APPLICATION_JSON).body(users, User.class);
  }
}
```

Finally, we will have to create a server where we can keep REST APIs. In the following code, our `Server` class will create one REST API to get users:

```
package com.packtpub.reactive;
import static org.springframework.http.MediaType.APPLICATION_JSON;
import static
org.springframework.web.reactive.function.server.RequestPredicates.GET;
import static
org.springframework.web.reactive.function.server.RequestPredicates.POST;
import static
org.springframework.web.reactive.function.server.RequestPredicates.accept;
import static
org.springframework.web.reactive.function.server.RequestPredicates.contentType;
import static
org.springframework.web.reactive.function.server.RequestPredicates.method;
import static
org.springframework.web.reactive.function.server.RequestPredicates.path;
import static
org.springframework.web.reactive.function.server.RouterFunctions.nest;
import static
org.springframework.web.reactive.function.server.RouterFunctions.route;
import static
org.springframework.web.reactive.function.server.RouterFunctions.toHttpHandler;
import java.io.IOException;
import org.springframework.http.HttpMethod;
import org.springframework.http.server.reactive.HttpHandler;
import org.springframework.http.server.reactive.ReactorHttpHandlerAdapter;
import org.springframework.web.reactive.function.server.RouterFunction;
import org.springframework.web.reactive.function.server.ServerResponse;
import reactor.ipc.netty.http.server.HttpServer;
public class Server {
  public static final String HOST = "localhost";
  public static final int PORT = 8081;
  public static void main(String[] args) throws InterruptedException,
IOException{
    Server server = new Server();
    server.startReactorServer();
    System.out.println("Press ENTER to exit.");
    System.in.read();
  }
  public void startReactorServer() throws InterruptedException {
    RouterFunction<ServerResponse> route = routingFunction();
    HttpHandler httpHandler = toHttpHandler(route);
    ReactorHttpHandlerAdapter adapter = new
ReactorHttpHandlerAdapter(httpHandler);
```

Flux and Mono (Reactor Support) in Spring

```
    HttpServer server = HttpServer.create(HOST, PORT);
    server.newHandler(adapter).block();
  }
  public RouterFunction<ServerResponse> routingFunction() {
    UserRepository repository = new UserRepositorySample();
    UserHandler handler = new UserHandler(repository);
    return nest (
        path("/user"),
        nest (
          accept(APPLICATION_JSON),
          route(GET("/{id}"), handler::getAllUsers)
          .andRoute(method(HttpMethod.GET), handler::getAllUsers)
        ).andRoute(POST("/").and(contentType(APPLICATION_JSON)),
handler::getAllUsers));
  }
}
```

We will discuss more about how we did this in upcoming chapters. Just make sure that you are able to understand that the code is working and you can see the output on the browser by accessing the API.

Run the `Server.class` and you will see the log:

Press ENTER to exit.

Now you can access the API in a browser/SoapUI/Postman, or any other client:

```
http://localhost:8081/user/
```

As we have used the `8081` port for the Reactive server, we will only have access to `8081` instead of `8080`:

```
[
  {
    "userid": 100,
    "username": "David"
  },
  {
    "userid": 101,
    "username": "John"
  },
  {
    "userid": 102,
    "username": "Kevin"
  },
]
```

Summary

So far, we have seen how to set up a Maven build to support our basic implementation of a web service. Also, we learned how Maven is helpful in third-party library management, as well as Spring Boot, and a basic Spring REST project. In upcoming chapters, we will discuss more about Spring REST endpoints and Reactor support.

4
CRUD Operations in Spring REST

In this chapter, we will go through basic **Create**, **Read**, **Update**, and **Delete** (**CRUD**) APIs in Spring 5 Reactive REST. After this chapter, you will be able to do a simple CRUD operations in Spring 5 with Reactor support.

In this chapter, we will cover the following methods:

- Mapping CRUD operations to HTTP methods
- Creating a user
- Updating a user
- Deleting a user
- Reading (selecting) a user

CRUD operations in Spring REST

In this chapter, we will go through User management in Spring 5 (with Reactive support). We will implement CRUD operations in User management.

HTTP methods

Based on HTTP 1.1 specifications, the following are method definitions:

- `GET`: This method gets the information mentioned in the URI. The `GET` method can be used for single or multiple items.
- `POST`: This method creates the item mentioned in the URI. Generally, the `POST` method will be used for item creation and more secured options. As the parameters are hidden in `POST`, it will be secure compared to the `GET` method.
- `DELETE`: This methods deletes the item in the requested URI.
- `PUT`: This method updates the item in the requested URI. According to the HTTP specifications, the server can create the item if the item is not available. However, this will be decided by the developer who designed the application.
- **Advanced HTTP methods**: Though we may not use advanced methods all the time, it will be good to know these methods, as they might be useful:
    - `HEAD`: This method gets meta information about the resource, not the resource itself, as a response. It will be used for caching purposes.
    - `TRACE`: This method is mostly used for debugging purposes where the contents of an HTTP request will be sent back to the requester.
    - `CONNECT`: This is used to open a tunnel and can be used for proxy purposes.
    - `OPTIONS`: This method is used to describe communication options for the target resource.

The following are HTTP method recommendations for our CRUD operations:

Operation	HTTP method
Create	`POST`
Read	`GET`
Update	`PUT`
Delete	`DELETE`

In the rest of the chapter, we will show how to build CRUD operations.

Reactive server initialization

Before jumping in to the endpoint, we will explore the structure of our files, including the initializer, handler, and repository.

The `Server` class for initializing our port `8081` is as follows:

```java
public class Server {
  public static final String HOST = "localhost";
  public static final int PORT = 8081;
  public static void main(String[] args) throws InterruptedException,
IOException{
    Server server = new Server();
    server.startReactorServer();
    System.out.println("Press ENTER to exit.");
    System.in.read();
  }
  public void startReactorServer() throws InterruptedException {
    RouterFunction<ServerResponse> route = routingFunction();
    HttpHandler httpHandler = toHttpHandler(route);
    ReactorHttpHandlerAdapter adapter = new
ReactorHttpHandlerAdapter(httpHandler);
    HttpServer server = HttpServer.create(HOST, PORT);
    server.newHandler(adapter).block();
  }
  public RouterFunction<ServerResponse> routingFunction() {
    // our Endpoints will be coming here
  }
}
```

In the preceding method, we created a `main` class. Inside the `main` method, we will initialize the server and start the server with the following code:

```java
Server server = new Server();
server.startReactorServer();
```

The preceding method will start the Reactor server. The Reactor server implementation is as follows:

```java
RouterFunction<ServerResponse> route = routingFunction();
HttpHandler httpHandler = toHttpHandler(route);
ReactorHttpHandlerAdapter adapter = new
ReactorHttpHandlerAdapter(httpHandler);
HttpServer server = HttpServer.create(HOST, PORT);
server.newHandler(adapter).block();
```

CRUD Operations in Spring REST

Let's go through this code later, as the concept is Reactive-based. Let's assume that this code works fine and we will move on, focusing on the endpoints.

The following is the method for mapping all REST endpoints for our CRUD operations:

```
public RouterFunction<ServerResponse> routingFunction() {
    // our Endpoints will be coming here
}
```

You might get errors on `UserRepository` and `UserHandler`. Let's fill these up now:

```
package com.packtpub.reactive;
public interface UserRepository {
    // repository functions will be coming here
}
```

In the preceding code, we have just added the `UserRepository` interface in our existing package `com.packtpub.reactive`. Later, we will introduce abstract methods for our business requirements.

Now, we can add a `UserHandler` class, and add the necessary things:

```
package com.packtpub.reactive;
// import statements
public class UserHandler {
    private final UserRepository userRepository;
    public UserHandler(UserRepository userRepository){
        this.userRepository = userRepository;
    }
}
```

In the preceding code, the `UserHandler` initializes the `UserRepository` instance in its constructor. If someone gets an instance of `UserHandler`, they will have to pass the `UserRepository` type to the `UserHandler` constructor. By doing this, `UserRepository` will always be forwarded to `UserHandler` to fulfill the business requirements.

Sample values in the repository

In order to use the repository, we will have to create a concrete class and fill in some values to test the `GET` operation. In the following method, we can do that:

```
package com.packtpub.reactive;
// import statements
public class UserRepositorySample implements UserRepository {
  // initiate Users
```

```
    private final Map<Integer, User> users = new HashMap<>();
    // fill dummy values for testing
    public UserRepositorySample() {
      this.users.put(100, new User(100, "David"));
      this.users.put(101, new User(101, "John"));
      this.users.put(102, new User(102, "Kevin"));
    }
}
```

In the preceding class, we just implemented `UserRepository` and filled in some sample values.

In order to simplify our code, we have used only application-based data storage, which means that once the application is restarted, our data will be reinitialized. In this case, we can't store any new data in our application. However, this will help us to focus on our main topics, such as Reactive and Spring 5, which are not related to persistence.

We can use this sample repository in the `routing` method:

```
public RouterFunction<ServerResponse> routingFunction() {
    UserRepository repository = new UserRepositorySample();
    UserHandler handler = new UserHandler(repository);
}
```

The preceding lines will insert dummy values in our repository. This will be enough for testing the `GET` operation.

getAllUsers – mapping

Inside the `routingFunction`, we will add our first endpoint for `getAllUsers`. At first, we will keep the `null` values in the handler to avoid errors in the code:

```
return nest (
    path("/user"),
    nest(
      accept(MediaType.ALL),
      route(GET("/"), null)
    )
);
```

The preceding `nest` method will be used to route to the right function, and it will also be used to group other routers. In the preceding method, we use `/user` in our path and we use `GET("/")` method as a router. Also, we use `MediaType.ALL` to accept all media ranges to simplify the code.

getAllUsers – implementation in the handler and repository

Here, we will define and implement the `getAllUsers` method in our repository. Also, we will call the `getAllUsers` method in the `main` class through `UserHandler`.

We will add an abstract method for the `getAllUsers` method in the `UserRepository` class:

```
Flux<User> getAllUsers();
```

Like any other interface and concrete class implementation, we will have to add the abstract method in our interface, in our case, `UserRespository`. The preceding code just adds `getAllUsers` in the `UserRepository` class.

In `UserRepositorySample` (the concrete class for `UserRepository`), we will implement the abstract method `getAllUsers`:

```
// this method will return all users
@Override
public Flux<User> getAllUsers() {
    return Flux.fromIterable(this.users.values());
}
```

In the preceding code, we have added the method `getAllUsers` and implemented the business logic. As we have already defined the users in the `UserRepositorySample` constructor, we just need to return the users. The `Flux` class has a method called `fromIterable`, which is used to get all users from our `UserRepositorySample`.

The `fromIterable` method will return a Flux that emits the items contained in our Java Collection interface. As Collection implements iterable interface, `fromIterable` will be the perfect method to return `Flux` in our case.

In the `UserHandler.java` file, we will add the code to get all users in Reactive. The following code will walk us through the necessary details:

```
public Mono<ServerResponse> getAllUsers(ServerRequest request){
  Flux<User> users = this.userRepository.getAllUsers();
    return ServerResponse.ok().contentType(APPLICATION_JSON).body(users, User.class);
}
```

In the preceding code, we will get all users from the repository in `Flux` and we will send them in the response in the JSON type. The server response content type is updated with `APPLICATION_JSON`.

Now is the time to add our first method, `getAllUsers`, in our routing method. Here, we will use only one routing method to map all REST APIs.

Finally, our routing function will look as follows in `Server.java`:

```java
public class Server {
    // existing code is hidden
    public RouterFunction<ServerResponse> routingFunction() {
        UserRepository repository = new UserRepositorySample();
        UserHandler handler = new UserHandler(repository);
        return nest (
            path("/user"),
            nest (
              accept(MediaType.ALL),
              route(GET("/"), handler::getAllUsers)
            )
        );
    }
}
```

In the preceding code, we created a `UserRepository` and forwarded it to our `UserHandler`. `UserHandler` will automatically call the `getAllUsers` method in `UserSampleRepository`. By calling the `getAllUsers` method of `UserHandler`, we will get all users from the sample repository class that we have implemented before.

Here, we are using the `nest` method and supplying parameters, such as the API path `GET("/")` and the media type. As the `nest` method accepts `RoutingFunction` as the second parameter, we can use more `nest` methods inside our basic `nest` methods. By using inner nesting methods, we have achieved the business requirement: our basic REST API starts from `"/user"` and basic get users API routing by `"/"`.

So, the basic API path `/user` will automatically call the `getAllUsers` method as it's implemented in the preceding code.

Testing the endpoint – getAllUsers

As we have finished out first API implementation, we can now test it by calling the following URI in the browser:

```
http://localhost:8081/user
```

You should get the following result:

```
[
  {
    userid: 100,
    username: "David"
  },
  {
    userid: 101,
    username: "John"
  },
  {
    userid: 102,
    username: "Kevin"
  }
]
```

You can also check the API in any REST client, like Postman/SoapUI or any other REST client.

getUser – implementation in the handler and repository

Here, we will define and implement the `getUser` method in our repository. Also, we will call the `getUser` method in the `main` class through `UserHandler`.

We will add an abstract method for the `getUser` method in the `UserRepository` class:

```
Mono<User> getUser(Integer id);
```

Here, we will add the code for the `getUser` method. You can see that we have used the `Mono` return type for single-resource access.

In the `UserRepositorySample` class (the concrete class for `UserRepository`), we will implement the abstract method `getUser`:

```
@Override
public Mono<User> getUser(Integer id){
    return Mono.justOrEmpty(this.users.get(id));
}
```

In the preceding code, we have retrieved the specific user by `id`. Also, we have mentioned that if the user is not available, the method should be asked to return an empty Mono.

In the `UserHandler` method, we will talk about how to handle the request and apply our business logic to get the response:

```
public Mono<ServerResponse> getUser(ServerRequest request){
    int userId = Integer.valueOf(request.pathVariable("id"));
    Mono<ServerResponse> notFound = ServerResponse.notFound().build();
    Mono<User> userMono = this.userRepository.getUser(userId);
    return userMono
        .flatMap(user ->
ServerResponse.ok().contentType(APPLICATION_JSON).body(fromObject(user)))
        .switchIfEmpty(notFound);
}
```

In the preceding code, we have just converted the string `id` to an integer in order to supply it to our `Repository` method (`getUser`). Once we receive the result from the `Repository`, we are just mapping it in to `Mono<ServerResponse>` with the `JSON` content type. Also, we use `switchIfEmpty` to send the proper response if no item is available. If the searching item is not available, it will simply return the empty `Mono` object as a response.

Finally, we will add `getUser` in our routing path, which is in `Server.java`:

```
public RouterFunction<ServerResponse> routingFunction() {
    UserRepository repository = new UserRepositorySample();
    UserHandler handler = new UserHandler(repository);
    return nest (
      path("/user"),
      nest (
        accept(MediaType.ALL),
        route(GET("/"), handler::getAllUsers)
      )
      .andRoute(GET("/{id}"), handler::getUser)
    );
}
```

In the preceding code, we have just added a new entry, `.andRoute(GET("/{id}"), handler::getUser)`, in our existing routing path. By doing so, we have added the `getUser` method and the corresponding REST API part to access a single user. After restarting the server, we should be able to use the REST API.

Testing the endpoint – getUser

As we have finished out first API implementation, we can now test it by calling the following URI in the browser using the `GET` method:

```
http://localhost:8081/user/100
```

You should get the following result:

```
{
    userid: 100,
    username: "David"
}
```

createUser – implementation in the handler and repository

Here, we will define and implement the `createUser` method in our repository. Also, we will call the `createUser` method in the `main` class through `UserHandler`.

We will add an abstract method for the `createUser` method in the `UserRepository` class:

```
Mono<Void> saveUser(Mono<User> userMono);
```

Here, we will talk about how to save the user by using the sample repository method.

In `UserRepositorySample` (the concrete class for `UserRepository`), we will implement the abstract method `createUser`:

```
@Override
public Mono<Void> saveUser(Mono<User> userMono) {
    return userMono.doOnNext(user -> {
      users.put(user.getUserid(), user);
      System.out.format("Saved %s with id %d%n", user, user.getUserid());
    }).thenEmpty(Mono.empty());
}
```

In the preceding code, we used `doOnNext` to save the user on the repository. Also, the method will return the empty `Mono` in the case of failure.

As we have added the `createUser` method in the repository, here we will follow up on our handler:

```
public Mono<ServerResponse> createUser(ServerRequest request) {
    Mono<User> user = request.bodyToMono(User.class);
    return ServerResponse.ok().build(this.userRepository.saveUser(user));
}
```

In the `UserHandler` class, we have created the `createUser` method to add a user through a handler. In the method, we extract the request into `Mono` by the `bodyToMono` method. Once the `user` is created, it will be forwarded to `UserRepository` to save the method.

Finally, we will add the REST API path to save the `user` in our existing routing function in `Server.java`:

```
public RouterFunction<ServerResponse> routingFunction() {
    UserRepository repository = new UserRepositorySample();
    UserHandler handler = new UserHandler(repository);
    return nest (
      path("/user"),
      nest(
        accept(MediaType.ALL),
        route(GET("/"), handler::getAllUsers)
      )
      .andRoute(GET("/{id}"), handler::getUser)
      .andRoute(POST("/").and(contentType(APPLICATION_JSON)), handler::createUser)
    );
}
```

Testing the endpoint – createUser

As we have finished out first API implementation, we can now test it by calling the following URI in the browser:

```
http://localhost:8081/user
```

CRUD Operations in Spring REST

As we can't use the `POST` method in a browser, we will test it in a REST API client, called Postman:

After adding the new user, you can check the results by calling the `getAllUsers` URI (`http://localhost:8081/user`).

> **Postman** is a REST client that can be used to build, test, and share REST API calls. Tools like these will be very helpful when we test our REST API without having to write code for testing.
>
> **SoapUI** is another REST client and can be used as an alternative to Postman.

updateUser – implementation in the handler and repository

Here, we will define and implement the `updateUser` method in our repository. Also, we will call the `updateUser` method in the main class through `UserHandler`.

[58]

We will add an abstract method for the updateUser method in the UserRepository class:

```
Mono<Void> updateUser(Mono<User> userMono);
```

In the UserRepositorySample class, we will add the logic to update the code. Here, we will use the userid as the key and the User object as the value to store in our map:

```
@;Override
public Mono<Void> updateUser(Mono<User> userMono) {
    return userMono.doOnNext(user -> {
      users.put(user.getUserid(), user);
      System.out.format("Saved %s with id %d%n", user, user.getUserid());
    }).thenEmpty(Mono.empty());
}
```

In the preceding code, we have updated the user by adding the specified user (from the request). Once the user is added in the list, the method will return Mono<Void>; otherwise, it will return the Mono.empty object.

As we have added the updateUser method in the repository, here we will follow up on our handler:

```
public Mono<ServerResponse> updateUser(ServerRequest request) {
    Mono<User> user = request.bodyToMono(User.class);
    return ServerResponse.ok().build(this.userRepository.saveUser(user));
}
```

In the preceding code, we have converting the user request to Mono<User> by calling the bodyToMono method. The bodyToMono method will extract the body into a Mono object, so it can be used for the saving option.

As we did with other API paths, we add the updateUser API in Server.java:

```
public RouterFunction<ServerResponse> routingFunction() {
    UserRepository repository = new UserRepositorySample();
    UserHandler handler = new UserHandler(repository);
    return nest (
      path("/user"),
      nest(
        accept(MediaType.ALL),
        route(GET("/"), handler::getAllUsers)
      )
        .andRoute(GET("/{id}"), handler::getUser)
        .andRoute(POST("/").and(contentType(APPLICATION_JSON)),
handler::createUser)
        .andRoute(PUT("/").and(contentType(APPLICATION_JSON)),
```

```
handler::updateUser)
    );
}
```

Testing the endpoint – updateUser

As we have finished out first API implementation, we can now test it by calling the URI `http://localhost:8081/user` in Postman or SoapUI, using the `PUT` method:

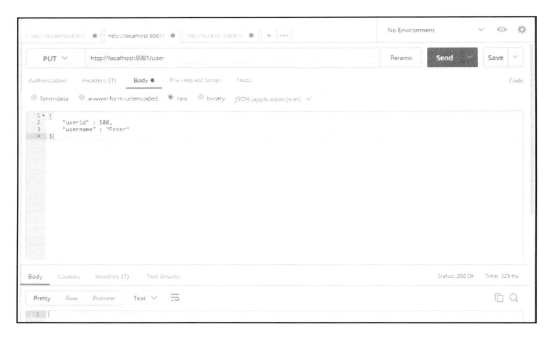

After updating the new user, you can check the results by calling the `getAllUsers` URI (`http://localhost:8081/user`).

deleteUser – implementation in the handler and repository

Here, we will define and implement the `deleteUser` method in our repository. Also, we will call the `deleteUser` method in the `main` class through `UserHandler`.

As usual, we will add an abstract method for the `deleteUser` method in the `UserRepository` class:

```
Mono<Void> deleteUser(Integer id);
```

In the `UserRepositorySample.java` file, we will add the `deleteUser` method to remove the specified user from the list:

```
@Override
public Mono<Void> deleteUser(Integer id) {
    users.remove(id);
    System.out.println("user : "+users);
    return Mono.empty();
}
```

In the preceding method, we simply remove the element from users and return an empty `Mono` object.

As we have added the `deleteUser` method in the repository, here we will follow up on our handler:

```
public Mono<ServerResponse> deleteUser(ServerRequest request) {
    int userId = Integer.valueOf(request.pathVariable("id"));
    return ServerResponse.ok().build(this.userRepository.deleteUser(userId));
}
```

Finally, we will add the REST API path to save the `user` in our existing routing function in `Server.java`:

```
public RouterFunction<ServerResponse> routingFunction() {
    UserRepository repository = new UserRepositorySample();
    UserHandler handler = new UserHandler(repository);
    return nest (
      path("/user"),
      nest(
        accept(MediaType.ALL),
        route(GET("/"), handler::getAllUsers)
      )
```

CRUD Operations in Spring REST

```
        .andRoute(GET("/{id}"), handler::getUser)
        .andRoute(POST("/").and(contentType(APPLICATION_JSON)),
handler::createUser)
        .andRoute(PUT("/").and(contentType(APPLICATION_JSON)),
handler::updateUser)
        .andRoute(DELETE("/{id}"), handler::deleteUser)
    );
}
```

Testing the endpoint – deleteUser

As we have finished out first API implementation, we can now test it by calling the URI `http://localhost:8081/user/100` in our client (Postman or SoapUI) using the DELETE method:

After deleting the new user, you can check the results by calling the `getAllUsers` URI (`http://localhost:8081/user`).

Summary

In this chapter, we have learned how to use Reactive support (Flux and Mono) and how to integrate our APIs with Reactive components. We have learned basic CRUD operations on Reactive-based REST APIs with the help of the Reactor server. Also, we have covered how to add routing options for our CRUD operations and talked a little bit about Flux and Mono implementations in our CRUD operations.

In the coming chapters, we will be focusing on Spring 5 REST (without Reactor support), as Spring Reactive libraries/APIs are still in unstable mode and haven't been used much in mainstream applications. Though the Spring team officially released support for Reactive, most business requirements are not clearly implemented and documented. Considering this situation, in upcoming chapters we will talk about Spring 5 without Reactive-related topics.

5
CRUD Operations in Plain REST (Without Reactive) and File Upload

In the last chapter, we explored a CRUD operation with Reactive support. As the Spring development team is still updating more Reactive entities, Reactive support hasn't reached their level yet. Though Spring 5 Reactive support is working fine, they still need to improve it to make it stable. After considering these pointers, we plan to avoid Reactive support in order to make it simple for you.

In this chapter, we will go through basic CRUD (Create, Read, Update, and Delete) APIs in Spring 5 (without Reactive) REST. After this chapter, you will be able to do a simple CRUD operation in Spring 5 without Reactive support. Also, we will talk about file upload options in Spring 5.

In this chapter, we will cover the following methods:

- Mapping CRUD operations to HTTP methods
- Creating a user
- Updating a user
- Deleting a user
- Reading (selecting) a user
- File uploads in Spring

Mapping CRUD operations to HTTP methods

In the last chapter, you saw CRUD operations in the controller. In this chapter, we will have the same CRUD operations; however, we've excluded all Reactive components.

Creating resources

To create basic Spring project resources, you can use Spring Initializr (https://start.spring.io/). In Spring Initializr, provide the necessary details:

Generate a **Maven Project** with **Java** and Spring Boot **1.5.9**.

Group: com.packtpub.restapp

Artifact: ticket-management

Search for dependencies: Select Web (Full Stack Web Development with Tomcat and Web MVC) dependency

After filling in the details, just click **Generate Project**; then it will create Spring basic resources in ZIP format. We can start using the project by importing them into Eclipse.

The Spring 5 POM file will look like this:

```
<?xml version="1.0" encoding="UTF-8"?>
<project xmlns="http://maven.apache.org/POM/4.0.0"
xmlns:xsi="http://www.w3.org/2001/XMLSchema-instance"
  xsi:schemaLocation="http://maven.apache.org/POM/4.0.0
http://maven.apache.org/xsd/maven-4.0.0.xsd">
  <modelVersion>4.0.0</modelVersion>
  <groupId>com.packtpub.restapp</groupId>
  <artifactId>ticket-management</artifactId>
  <version>0.0.1-SNAPSHOT</version>
  <packaging>jar</packaging>
  <name>ticket-management</name>
  <description>Demo project for Spring Boot</description>
  <parent>
    <groupId>org.springframework.boot</groupId>
    <artifactId>spring-boot-starter-parent</artifactId>
    <version>1.5.9.RELEASE</version>
    <relativePath/> <!-- lookup parent from repository -->
  </parent>
  <properties>
```

```xml
      <project.build.sourceEncoding>UTF-8</project.build.sourceEncoding>
   <project.reporting.outputEncoding>UTF-8</project.reporting.outputEncoding>
    </properties>
    <dependencies>
      <dependency>
        <groupId>org.springframework.boot</groupId>
        <artifactId>spring-boot-starter-web</artifactId>
      </dependency>
      <dependency>
        <groupId>org.springframework.boot</groupId>
        <artifactId>spring-boot-starter-test</artifactId>
        <scope>test</scope>
      </dependency>
    </dependencies>
    <build>
      <plugins>
        <plugin>
          <groupId>org.springframework.boot</groupId>
          <artifactId>spring-boot-maven-plugin</artifactId>
        </plugin>
      </plugins>
    </build>
</project>
```

Let's remove the parent to simplify the POM:

```xml
<parent>
   <groupId>org.springframework.boot</groupId>
   <artifactId>spring-boot-starter-parent</artifactId>
   <version>1.5.9.RELEASE</version>
   <relativePath/> <!-- lookup parent from repository -->
</parent>
```

As we removed the parent, we may need to add the version in all of our dependencies. Let's add the version in our dependencies:

```xml
<dependencies>
    <dependency>
       <groupId>org.springframework.boot</groupId>
       <artifactId>spring-boot-starter-web</artifactId>
       <version>1.5.9.RELEASE</version>
    </dependency>
    <dependency>
       <groupId>org.springframework.boot</groupId>
       <artifactId>spring-boot-starter-test</artifactId>
       <scope>test</scope>
       <version>1.5.9.RELEASE</version>
    </dependency>
```

CRUD Operations in Plain REST (Without Reactive) and File Upload

```
    </dependencies>
```

As the dependency artifact `spring-boot-starter-web` version 1.5.9 is based on Spring 4.3.11, we will have to upgrade to Spring 5. Let's clean and upgrade our POM file to bring in Spring 5 updates:

```xml
<?xml version="1.0" encoding="UTF-8"?>
<project xmlns="http://maven.apache.org/POM/4.0.0"
xmlns:xsi="http://www.w3.org/2001/XMLSchema-instance"
   xsi:schemaLocation="http://maven.apache.org/POM/4.0.0
http://maven.apache.org/xsd/maven-4.0.0.xsd">
   <modelVersion>4.0.0</modelVersion>
   <groupId>com.packtpub.restapp</groupId>
   <artifactId>ticket-management</artifactId>
   <version>0.0.1-SNAPSHOT</version>
   <packaging>jar</packaging>
   <name>ticket-management</name>
   <description>Demo project for Spring Boot</description>
   <properties>
      <project.build.sourceEncoding>UTF-8</project.build.sourceEncoding>
<project.reporting.outputEncoding>UTF-8</project.reporting.outputEncoding>
   </properties>
   <dependencies>
      <dependency>
         <groupId>org.springframework.boot</groupId>
         <artifactId>spring-boot-starter-web</artifactId>
         <version>1.5.9.RELEASE</version>
      </dependency>
      <dependency>
         <groupId>org.springframework.boot</groupId>
         <artifactId>spring-boot-starter-test</artifactId>
         <scope>test</scope>
         <version>1.5.9.RELEASE</version>
      </dependency>
   </dependencies>
   <build>
      <plugins>
         <plugin>
            <groupId>org.springframework.boot</groupId>
            <artifactId>spring-boot-maven-plugin</artifactId>
         </plugin>
      </plugins>
   </build>
</project>
```

You can see Spring 5-related dependencies in the preceding POM file. Let's test them with the REST endpoint. First, create a Spring Boot main file to initialize Spring Boot:

```
@SpringBootApplication
public class TicketManagementApplication {
  public static void main(String[] args) {
    SpringApplication.run(TicketManagementApplication.class, args);
  }
}
```

You can start running the Spring Boot on Eclipse by right-clicking the project and selecting **Run As** | **Spring Boot App**. If you do this, you will see logs in the Eclipse console.

If you don't see the console, you can get it via **Window** | **Show View** | **Console**.

The following is a sample log. You may not see an exact match; however, you will get an idea of how the server running log will look:

```
  .   ____          _            __ _ _
 /\\ / ___'_ __ _ _(_)_ __  __ _ \ \ \ \
( ( )\___ | '_ | '_| | '_ \/ _` | \ \ \ \
 \\/  ___)| |_)| | | | | || (_| |  ) ) ) )
  '  |____| .__|_| |_|_| |_\__, | / / / /
 =========|_|==============|___/=/_/_/_/
 :: Spring Boot ::        (v1.5.7.RELEASE)

2017-11-05 15:49:21.380  INFO 8668 --- [    main]
c.p.restapp.TicketManagementApplication  : Starting
TicketManagementApplication on DESKTOP-6JP2FNB with PID 8668 (C:\d\spring-
book-sts-space\ticket-management\target\classes started by infoadmin in
C:\d\spring-book-sts-space\ticket-management)
2017-11-05 15:49:21.382  INFO 8668 --- [    main]
c.p.restapp.TicketManagementApplication  : No active profile set, falling
back to default profiles: default
2017-11-05 15:49:21.421  INFO 8668 --- [    main]
ationConfigEmbeddedWebApplicationContext : Refreshing
org.springframework.boot.context.embedded.AnnotationConfigEmbeddedWebApplic
ationContext@5ea434c8: startup date [Sun Nov 05 15:49:21 EST 2017]; root of
context hierarchy
2017-11-05 15:49:22.205  INFO 8668 --- [    main]
s.b.c.e.t.TomcatEmbeddedServletContainer : Tomcat initialized with port(s):
8080 (http)
2017-11-05 15:49:22.213  INFO 8668 --- [    main]
o.apache.catalina.core.StandardService   : Starting service [Tomcat]
```

CRUD Operations in Plain REST (Without Reactive) and File Upload

```
...
..
...
...
2017-11-05 15:49:22.834 INFO 8668 --- [ main]
o.s.j.e.a.AnnotationMBeanExporter : Registering beans for JMX exposure on
startup
2017-11-05 15:49:22.881 INFO 8668 --- [ main]
s.b.c.e.t.TomcatEmbeddedServletContainer : Tomcat started on port(s): 8080
(http)
```

You should see `Tomcat started on port(s): 8080` in the last lines of the log.

When you check the URI `http://localhost:8080`, you will see the following error:

```
Whitelabel Error Page

This application has no explicit mapping for /error, so you are seeing this
as a fallback.

Sun Nov {current date}
There was an unexpected error (type=Not Found, status=404).
No message available
```

The preceding error is saying that there is no corresponding URI configured in the application. Let's fix this issue by creating a controller called `HomeController` under the `com.packtpub.restapp` package:

```
package com.packtpub.restapp;
import java.util.LinkedHashMap;
import java.util.Map;
import org.springframework.web.bind.annotation.RequestMapping;
import org.springframework.web.bind.annotation.ResponseBody;
import org.springframework.web.bind.annotation.RestController;
@RestController
@RequestMapping("/")
public class HomeController {
  @ResponseBody
  @RequestMapping("")
  public Map<String, Object> test(){
    Map<String, Object> map = new LinkedHashMap<>();
    map.put("result", "Aloha");
    return map;
  }
}
```

In the preceding code, we created a dummy controller called `HomeController` with a simple map as a result. Also, we added the new controller we need to have these classes autoscanned by our main application, in our case the `TicketManagementApplication` class. We will tell them by adding `@ComponentScan("com.packtpub")` in the main class. Finally, our main class will look like the following:

```
package com.packtpub.restapp.ticketmanagement;
import org.springframework.boot.SpringApplication;
import org.springframework.boot.autoconfigure.SpringBootApplication;
import org.springframework.context.annotation.ComponentScan;
@ComponentScan("com.packtpub")
@SpringBootApplication
public class TicketManagementApplication {
  public static void main(String[] args) {
    SpringApplication.run(TicketManagementApplication.class, args);
  }
}
```

When you restart the Spring Boot App, you will see the REST endpoint working (`localhost:8080`):

```
{
  result: "Aloha"
}
```

CRUD operation in Spring 5 (without Reactive)

Let's perform user CRUD operations. As we have discussed CRUD concepts before, here we will only discuss User management on Spring 5 (without Reactive support). Let's fill in all dummy methods for CRUD endpoints. In here, we can create `UserContoller` and fill in all methods for CRUD user operations:

```
package com.packtpub.restapp;
import java.util.LinkedHashMap;
import java.util.Map;
import org.springframework.web.bind.annotation.PathVariable;
import org.springframework.web.bind.annotation.RequestMapping;
import org.springframework.web.bind.annotation.RequestMethod;
import org.springframework.web.bind.annotation.ResponseBody;
import org.springframework.web.bind.annotation.RestController;
@RestController
@RequestMapping("/user")
```

CRUD Operations in Plain REST (Without Reactive) and File Upload

```java
public class UserController {
  @ResponseBody
  @RequestMapping("")
  public Map<String, Object> getAllUsers(){
    Map<String, Object> map = new LinkedHashMap<>();
    map.put("result", "Get All Users Implementation");
    return map;
  }
  @ResponseBody
  @RequestMapping("/{id}")
  public Map<String, Object> getUser(@PathVariable("id") Integer id){
    Map<String, Object> map = new LinkedHashMap<>();
    map.put("result", "Get User Implementation");
    return map;
  }
  @ResponseBody
  @RequestMapping(value = "", method = RequestMethod.POST)
  public Map<String, Object> createUser(){
    Map<String, Object> map = new LinkedHashMap<>();
    map.put("result", "Create User Implementation");
    return map;
  }
  @ResponseBody
  @RequestMapping(value = "", method = RequestMethod.PUT)
  public Map<String, Object> updateUser(){
    Map<String, Object> map = new LinkedHashMap<>();
    map.put("result", "Update User Implementation");
    return map;
  }
  @ResponseBody
  @RequestMapping(value = "", method = RequestMethod.DELETE)
  public Map<String, Object> deleteUser(){
    Map<String, Object> map = new LinkedHashMap<>();
    map.put("result", "Delete User Implementation");
    return map;
  }
}
```

We have filled the basic endpoints for all CRUD operations. If you call them on Postman with proper methods such as GET, POST, PUT, and DELETE, you will see the result mentioning the appropriate messages.

For example, for the getAllUsers API (localhost:8080/user), you will get:

```
{
  result: "Get All Users Implementation"
}
```

getAllUsers – implementation

Let's implement the `getAllUsers` API. For this API, we may need to create a model class called `User` under the package `com.packtpub.model`:

```
package com.packtpub.model;
public class User {
  private Integer userid;
  private String username;
  public User(Integer userid, String username){
    this.userid = userid;
    this.username = username;
  }
  // getter and setter methods
}
```

Now, we will add code for the `getAllUsers` implementation. As this is business logic, we will create a separate `UserService` and `UserServiceImpl` class. By doing this, we can keep the business logic in a different place to avoid code complexity.

The `UserService` interface will look as follows:

```
package com.packtpub.service;
import java.util.List;
import com.packtpub.model.User;
public interface UserService {
  List<User> getAllUsers();
}
```

The `UserServiceImpl` class implementation is as follows:

```
package com.packtpub.service;
import java.util.LinkedList;
import java.util.List;
import org.springframework.stereotype.Service;
import com.packtpub.model.User;
@Service
public class UserServiceImpl implements UserService {
  @Override
  public List<User> getAllUsers() {
    return this.users;
  }
  // Dummy users
  public static List<User> users;
  public UserServiceImpl() {
    users = new LinkedList<>();
    users.add(new User(100, "David"));
```

```
        users.add(new User(101, "Peter"));
        users.add(new User(102, "John"));
    }
}
```

In the preceding implementation, we created dummy users in the constructor. When the class is initialized by a Spring configuration, these users will be added to the list.

The `UserController` class for calling the `getAllUsers` method is as follows:

```
@Autowired
UserService userSevice;
@ResponseBody
@RequestMapping("")
public List<User> getAllUsers(){
    return userSevice.getAllUsers();
}
```

In the preceding code, we have called the `getAllUsers` method by autowiring it in the controller file. `@Autowired` will do all the instantiation magic behind the scenes.

If you run the application now, you may face the following error:

```
***************************
APPLICATION FAILED TO START
***************************

Description:

Field userSevice in com.packtpub.restapp.UserController required a bean of
type 'com.packtpub.service.UserService' that could not be found.


Action:

Consider defining a bean of type 'com.packtpub.service.UserService' in your
configuration.
```

The reason behind this error is that your application is not able to identify `UserService`, as it is in a different package. We can fix this issue by adding `@ComponentScan("com.packtpub")` in the `TicketManagementApplication` class. This will identify all `@service` and other beans in different sub-packages:

```
@ComponentScan("com.packtpub")
@SpringBootApplication
public class TicketManagementApplication {
    public static void main(String[] args) {
```

```
        SpringApplication.run(TicketManagementApplication.class, args);
    }
}
```

Now you can see the result when you call the API (http://localhost:8080/user):

```
[
    {
        userid: 100,
        username: "David"
    },
    {
        userid: 101,
        username: "Peter"
    },
    {
        userid: 102,
        username: "John"
    }
]
```

getUser – implementation

Like we did earlier in Chapter 4, *CRUD Operations in Spring REST* we are going to implement getUser business logic in this section. Let's add the getUser method here by using Java 8 Streams.

The UserService interface will look as follows:

```
User getUser(Integer userid);
```

The UserServiceImpl class implementation is as follows:

```
@Override
public User getUser(Integer userid) {
    return users.stream()
        .filter(x -> x.getUserid() == userid)
        .findAny()
        .orElse(new User(0, "Not Available"));
}
```

In the previous `getUser` method implementation, we used Java 8 Streams and lambda expressions to get the user by `userid`. Instead of using the traditional `for` loop, lambda expressions make it easier to fetch the details. In the preceding code, we check the user by filter criteria. If the user is matched, it will return the specific user; otherwise, it will create a dummy user with the `"Not available"` message.

The `UserController` class for the `getUser` method is as follows:

```
@ResponseBody
@RequestMapping("/{id}")
public User getUser(@PathVariable("id") Integer id){
  return userSevice.getUser(100);
}
```

You can verify the API by accessing `http://localhost:8080/user/100` in the client (use Postman or SoapUI to test it):

```
{
  userid: 100,
  username: "David"
}
```

createUser – implementation

Now we can add the code for creating a user option.

The `UserService` interface will look as follows:

```
void createUser(Integer userid, String username);
```

The `UserServiceImpl` class implementation is as follows:

```
@Override
public void createUser(Integer userid, String username) {
   User user = new User(userid, username);
   this.users.add(user);
}
```

The `UserController` class for the `createUser` method is as follows:

```
@ResponseBody
  @RequestMapping(value = "", method = RequestMethod.POST)
    public Map<String, Object> createUser(
      @RequestParam(value="userid") Integer userid,
      @RequestParam(value="username") String username
```

```
){
Map<String, Object> map = new LinkedHashMap<>();
userSevice.createUser(userid, username);
map.put("result", "added");
return map;
}
```

The preceding code will add the user in our map. Here, we have used `userid` and `username` as method parameters. You can view the `userid` and `username` in the following API call:

When you call this method using SoapUI/Postman, you will get the following result. In this case, we used parameters (`userid`, `username`) instead of JSON input. This is just to simplify the process:

```
{"result": "added"}
```

updateUser – implementation

Now we can add the code for the update user option.

The `UserService` interface will look as follows:

```
void updateUser(Integer userid, String username);
```

The `UserServiceImpl` class implementation is as follows:

```
@Override
public void updateUser(Integer userid, String username) {
    users.stream()
        .filter(x -> x.getUserid() == userid)
        .findAny()
        .orElseThrow(() -> new RuntimeException("Item not found"))
        .setUsername(username);
}
```

In the preceding method, we have used a Java Streams-based implementation to update the user. We simply apply the filter and check for whether the user is available or not. If the `userid` is not matched, it will throw `RuntimeException`. If the user is available, we will get the corresponding user, and then we update `username`.

The `UserController` class for the `updateUser` method is as follows:

```
@ResponseBody
  @RequestMapping(value = "", method = RequestMethod.PUT)
  public Map<String, Object> updateUser(
      @RequestParam(value="userid") Integer userid,
      @RequestParam(value="username") String username
    ){
    Map<String, Object> map = new LinkedHashMap<>();
    userSevice.updateUser(userid, username);
    map.put("result", "updated");
    return map;
  }
```

We will try to update `username` from `David` to `Sammy` on `userid` with value `100`. We can check the API details from the following screenshot:

When we call this API (the UPDATE method) using the SoapUI/Postman extension (http://localhost:8080/user), we will get the following result:

{"result": "updated"}

You can check the result by checking the getAllUsers API (the GET method) in the Postman extension (http://localhost:8080/user); you will get the following result:

```
[
  {
    "userid": 100,
    "username": "Sammy"
  },
  {
    "userid": 101,
    "username": "Peter"
  },
  {
    "userid": 102,
    "username": "John"
  },
  {
    "userid": 104,
    "username": "Kevin"
  }
]
```

deleteUser – implementation

Now we can add the code for the `deleteUser` option.

The `UserService` interface will look as follows:

```
void deleteUser(Integer userid);
```

The `UserServiceImpl` class implementation is as follows:

```
@Override
public void deleteUser(Integer userid) {
   users.removeIf((User u) -> u.getUserid() == userid);
}
```

The `UserController` class for the `deleteUser` method is as follows:

```
@ResponseBody
@RequestMapping(value = "/{id}", method = RequestMethod.DELETE)
public Map<String, Object> deleteUser(
      @PathVariable("id") Integer userid) {
   Map<String, Object> map = new LinkedHashMap<>();
   userSevice.deleteUser(userid);
   map.put("result", "deleted");
   return map;
}
```

When you call this API (the `DELETE` method) using the Postman extension (`http://localhost:8080/user/100`), you will get the following result:

```
{"result": "deleted"}
```

You can also check the `getAllUsers` method to verify that you have deleted the user.

File uploads – REST API

File uploading becomes very easy with the support of the `NIO` libraries and Spring's `MultipartFile` options. Here, we will add the code for file uploading.

The `FileUploadService` interface will look as follows:

```
package com.packtpub.service;
import org.springframework.web.multipart.MultipartFile;
public interface FileUploadService {
   void uploadFile(MultipartFile file) throws IOException;
}
```

In the preceding code, we just defined the method to let the concrete class (implementation class) override our method. We used `MultipartFile` here to forward a file, such as a media file to fulfill our business logic.

The `FileUploadServerImpl` class implementation is as follows:

```
package com.packtpub.service;
import java.io.IOException;
import java.nio.file.Files;
import java.nio.file.Path;
import java.nio.file.Paths;
import java.nio.file.StandardCopyOption;
import org.springframework.stereotype.Service;
import org.springframework.util.StringUtils;
import org.springframework.web.multipart.MultipartFile;
@Service
public class FileUploadServerImpl implements FileUploadService {
   private Path location;
   public FileUploadServerImpl() throws IOException {
      location = Paths.get("c:/test/");
      Files.createDirectories(location);
   }
   @Override
   public void uploadFile(MultipartFile file) throws IOException {
      String fileName = StringUtils.cleanPath(file.getOriginalFilename());
      if (fileName.isEmpty()) {
         throw new IOException("File is empty " + fileName);
      } try {
         Files.copy(file.getInputStream(),
               this.location.resolve(fileName),
               StandardCopyOption.REPLACE_EXISTING);
      } catch (IOException e) {
         throw new IOException("File Upload Error : " + fileName);
      }
   }
}
```

CRUD Operations in Plain REST (Without Reactive) and File Upload

In the preceding code, we set the location in the constructor itself, so when the Spring Boot App is initialized, it will set the correct path; if needed, it will create a specific folder on the mentioned location.

In the `uploadFile` method, we get the files and clean them first. We use a Spring utility class called `StringUtils` to clean the file path. You can see the cleaning process here:

```
String fileName = StringUtils.cleanPath(file.getOriginalFilename());
```

If the file is empty, we simply throw an exception. You can check the exception here:

```
if(fileName.isEmpty()){
   throw new IOException("File is empty " + fileName);
}
```

Then comes the real file upload logic! We just use the `Files.copy` method to copy the file from the client to the server location. If any error happens, we throw `RuntimeException`:

```
try {
    Files.copy(
       file.getInputStream(), this.location.resolve(fileName),
       StandardCopyOption.REPLACE_EXISTING
    );
} catch (IOException e) {
    throw new IOException("File Upload Error : " + fileName);
}
```

As the main implementation is done by the concrete class, the controller just passes the `MultipartFile` to the service. We have used the `POST` method in here, as it will be the perfect method to upload the file. Also, you can see that we used the `@Autowired` option to use the `service` method.

The `FileController` class for the `uploadFile` method is as follows:

```
package com.packtpub.restapp;
import java.io.IOException;
import java.util.LinkedHashMap;
import java.util.Map;
import org.springframework.beans.factory.annotation.Autowired;
import org.springframework.web.bind.annotation.RequestMapping;
import org.springframework.web.bind.annotation.RequestMethod;
import org.springframework.web.bind.annotation.RequestParam;
import org.springframework.web.bind.annotation.ResponseBody;
import org.springframework.web.bind.annotation.RestController;
import org.springframework.web.multipart.MultipartFile;
import com.packtpub.service.FileUploadService;
```

```
@RestController
@RequestMapping("/file")
public class FileController {
  @Autowired
  FileUploadService fileUploadSevice;
  @ResponseBody
  @RequestMapping(value = "/upload", method = RequestMethod.POST)
  public Map<String, Object> uploadFile(@RequestParam("file") MultipartFile file) {
    Map<String, Object> map = new LinkedHashMap<>();
    try {
      fileUploadSevice.uploadFile(file);
      map.put("result", "file uploaded");
    } catch (IOException e) {
      map.put("result", "error while uploading : "+e.getMessage());
    }
    return map;
  }
}
```

Testing the file upload

You can create an HTML file as follows and test the file upload API. You can also use any REST client to test this. I have given you this HTML file to simplify the testing process:

```
<!DOCTYPE html>
<html>
<body>
<form action="http://localhost:8080/file/upload" method="post" enctype="multipart/form-data">
    Select image to upload:
    <input type="file" name="file" id="file">
    <input type="submit" value="Upload Image" name="submit">
</form>
</body>
</html>
```

Summary

In this chapter, we have covered CRUD operations in Spring 5 (without Reactive support) by starting with basic resources and customizing them. Also, we have learned how to upload a file in Spring. In the next chapter, we will learn more about Spring Security and JWT (JSON Web Token).

6
Spring Security and JWT (JSON Web Token)

In this chapter, we will acquire a simple understanding of Spring Security and we will also talk about **JSON Web Token (JWT)** and how to use JWTs in our web service calls. This will also include JWT creation.

In this chapter, we will cover the following:

- Spring Security
- JSON Web Token (JWT)
- How to generate JWTs in web services
- How to access and retrieve information from JWTs in a web service
- How to restrict web service calls by adding JWT security

Spring Security

Spring Security is a powerful authentication and authorization framework, which will help us to provide a secure application. By using Spring Security, we can keep all of our REST APIs secured and accessible only by authenticated and authorized calls.

Authentication and authorization

Let's look at an example to explain this. Assume you have a library with many books. Authentication will provide a key to enter the library; however, authorization will give you permission to take a book. Without a key, you can't even enter the library. Even though you have a key to the library, you will be allowed to take only a few books.

JSON Web Token (JWT)

Spring Security can be applied in many forms, including XML configurations using powerful libraries such as JWT. As most companies use JWT in their security, we will focus more on JWT-based security than simple Spring Security, which can be configured in XML.

JWT tokens are URL-safe and web browser-compatible especially for **Single Sign-On** (**SSO**) contexts. JWT has three parts:

- Header
- Payload
- Signature

The header part decides which algorithm should be used to generate the token. While authenticating, the client has to save the JWT, which is returned by the server. Unlike traditional session creation approaches, this process doesn't need to store any cookies on the client side. JWT authentication is stateless as the client state is never saved on a server.

JWT dependency

To use JWT in our application, we may need to use the Maven dependency. The following dependency should be added in the pom.xml file. You can get the Maven dependency from: https://mvnrepository.com/artifact/javax.xml.bind.

We have used version 2.3.0 of the Maven dependency in our application:

```xml
<dependency>
    <groupId>javax.xml.bind</groupId>
    <artifactId>jaxb-api</artifactId>
    <version>2.3.0</version>
</dependency>
```

As Java 9 doesn't include `DataTypeConverter` in their bundle, we need to add the preceding configuration to work with `DataTypeConverter`. We will cover `DataTypeConverter` in the following section.

Creating a JWT token

To create a token, we have added an abstract method called `createToken` in our `SecurityService` interface. This interface will tell the implementing class that it has to create a complete method for `createToken`. In the `createToken` method, we will use only the subject and expiry time as these two options are important when creating a token.

At first, we will create an abstract method in the `SecurityService` interface. The concrete class (whoever implements the `SecurityService` interface) has to implement the method in their class:

```
public interface SecurityService {
  String createToken(String subject, long ttlMillis);
 // other methods
}
```

In the preceding code, we defined the method for token creation in the interface.

`SecurityServiceImpl` is the concrete class that implements the abstract method of the `SecurityService` interface by applying the business logic. The following code will explain how JWT will be created by using the subject and expiry time:

```
private static final String secretKey= "4C8kum4LxyKWYLM78sKdXrzbBjDCFyfX";
@Override
public String createToken(String subject, long ttlMillis) {
    if (ttlMillis <= 0) {
       throw new RuntimeException("Expiry time must be greater than Zero :["+ttlMillis+"] ");
    }
    // The JWT signature algorithm we will be using to sign the token
    SignatureAlgorithm signatureAlgorithm = SignatureAlgorithm.HS256;
    byte[] apiKeySecretBytes = DatatypeConverter.parseBase64Binary(secretKey);
    Key signingKey = new SecretKeySpec(apiKeySecretBytes, signatureAlgorithm.getJcaName());
    JwtBuilder builder = Jwts.builder()
        .setSubject(subject)
        .signWith(signatureAlgorithm, signingKey);
    long nowMillis = System.currentTimeMillis();
```

```
        builder.setExpiration(new Date(nowMillis + ttlMillis));
        return builder.compact();
}
```

The preceding code creates the token for the subject. Here, we have hardcoded the secret key `"4C8kum4LxyKWYLM78sKdXrzbBjDCFyfX"` to simplify the token creation process. If needed, we can keep the secret key inside the properties file to avoid hard code in the Java code.

At first, we verify whether the time is greater than zero. If not, we throw the exception right away. We are using the SHA-256 algorithm as it is used in most applications.

Secure Hash Algorithm (SHA) is a cryptographic hash function. The cryptographic hash is in the text form of a data file. The SHA-256 algorithm generates an almost-unique, fixed-size 256-bit hash. SHA-256 is one of the more reliable hash functions.

We have hardcoded the secret key in this class. We can also store the key in the `application.properties` file. However to simplify the process, we have hardcoded it:

```
private static final String secretKey= "4C8kum4LxyKWYLM78sKdXrzbBjDCFyfX";
```

We are converting the string key to a byte array and then passing it to a Java class, `SecretKeySpec`, to get a `signingKey`. This key will be used in the token builder. Also, while creating a signing key, we use JCA, the name of our signature algorithm.

Java Cryptography Architecture (JCA) was introduced by Java to support modern cryptography techniques.

We use the `JwtBuilder` class to create the token and set the expiration time for it. The following code defines the token creation and expiry time setting option:

```
JwtBuilder builder = Jwts.builder()
        .setSubject(subject)
        .signWith(signatureAlgorithm, signingKey);
long nowMillis = System.currentTimeMillis();
builder.setExpiration(new Date(nowMillis + ttlMillis));
```

We will have to pass time in milliseconds while calling this method as the `setExpiration` takes only milliseconds.

Finally, we have to call the `createToken` method in our `HomeController`. Before calling the method, we will have to autowire the `SecurityService` as follows:

```
@Autowired
SecurityService securityService;
```

The `createToken` call is coded as follows. We take the subject as the parameter. To simplify the process, we have hardcoded the expiry time as 2 * 1000 * 60 (two minutes).

HomeController.java:

```
@Autowired
SecurityService securityService;
@ResponseBody
  @RequestMapping("/security/generate/token")
    public Map<String, Object> generateToken(@RequestParam(value="subject")
String subject){
      String token = securityService.createToken(subject, (2 * 1000 * 60));
      Map<String, Object> map = new LinkedHashMap<>();
      map.put("result", token);
      return map;
    }
```

Generating a token

We can test the token by calling the API in a browser or any REST client. By calling this API, we can create a token. This token will be used for user authentication-like purposes.

Sample API for creating a token is as follows:

```
http://localhost:8080/security/generate/token?subject=one
```

Here we have used `one` as a subject. We can see the token in the following result. This is how the token will be generated for all the subjects we pass to the API:

```
{
  result:
"eyJhbGciOiJIUzI1NiJ9.eyJzdWIiOiJvbmUiLCJleHAiOjE1MDk5MzY2ODF9.GknKcywiI-
G4-R2bRmBOsjomujP0MxZqdawrB8TO3P4"
}
```

 JWT is a string that has three parts, each separated by a dot (.). Each section is base-64 encoded. The first section is the header, which gives a clue about the algorithm used to sign the JWT. The second section is the body, and the final section is the signature.

Getting a subject from a JWT token

So far, we have created a JWT token. Here, we are going to decode the token and get the subject from it. In a future section, we will talk about how to decode and get the subject from the token.

As usual, we have to define the method to get the subject. We will define the `getSubject` method in `SecurityService`.

Here, we will create an abstract method called `getSubject` in the `SecurityService` interface. Later, we will implement this method in our concrete class:

```
String getSubject(String token);
```

In our concrete class, we will implement the `getSubject` method and add our code in the `SecurityServiceImpl` class. We can use the following code to get the subject from the token:

```
@Override
public String getSubject(String token) {
   Claims claims = Jwts.parser()
.setSigningKey(DatatypeConverter.parseBase64Binary(secretKey))
         .parseClaimsJws(token).getBody();
   return claims.getSubject();
}
```

In the preceding method, we use the `Jwts.parser` to get the `claims`. We set a signing key by converting the secret key to binary and then passing it to a parser. Once we get the `Claims`, we can simply get the subject by calling `getSubject`.

Finally, we can call the method in our controller and pass the generated token to get the subject. You can check the following code, where the controller is calling the `getSubject` method and returning the subject in the `HomeController.java` file:

```
@ResponseBody
@RequestMapping("/security/get/subject")
public Map<String, Object> getSubject(@RequestParam(value="token") String token){
    String subject = securityService.getSubject(token);
    Map<String, Object> map = new LinkedHashMap<>();
    map.put("result", subject);
    return map;
}
```

Getting a subject from a token

Previously, we created the code to get the token. Here we will test the method we created previously by calling the get subject API. By calling the REST API, we will get the subject that we passed earlier.

Sample API:

```
http://localhost:8080/security/get/subject?token=eyJhbGciOiJIUzI1NiJ9.eyJzd
WIiOiJvbmUiLCJleHAiOjE1MDk5MzY2ODF9.GknKcywiI-G4-
R2bRmBOsjomujP0MxZqdawrB8TO3P4
```

Since we used `one` as the subject when creating the token by calling the `generateToken` method, we will get "one" in the `getSubject` method:

```
{
  result: "one"
}
```

 Usually, we attach the token in the headers; however, to avoid complexity, we have provided the result. Also, we have passed the token as a parameter to get the subject. You may not need to do it the same way in a real application. This is only for demo purposes.

Summary

In this chapter, we have discussed Spring Security and JWT token-based security to get and decode the token. In future chapters, we will discuss how to use the token in AOP and restrict the API call by using a JWT token.

7
Testing RESTful Web Services

In previous chapters, we have discussed how to create a REST API and apply the business logic inside our REST APIs and service methods. However, in order to be sure of our business logic, we may need to write proper test cases and use other testing methods. Testing our REST APIs will help us keep our application clean and functional when it is deployed in production. The more we write unit test cases or other testing methods, the better it is for us to maintain our application in the future.

In this chapter, we will discuss the following testing strategies for our sample RESTful web services:

- JUnit testing on Spring controllers
- MockMvc (mocking on controllers)
- Postman REST client
- SoapUI REST client
- jsoup reader as a client

JUnit

JUnit is the easiest and the most preferred testing framework for Java and Spring applications. By writing JUnit test cases for our application, we can improve the quality of our application and also avoid buggy situations.

Here, we will discuss a simple JUnit test case, which is calling the `getAllUsers` method in `userService`. We can check the following code:

```
@RunWith(SpringRunner.class)
@SpringBootTest
public class UserTests {
```

```
    @Autowired
    UserService userSevice;
    @Test
    public void testAllUsers(){
       List<User> users = userSevice.getAllUsers();
       assertEquals(3, users.size());
    }
}
```

In the preceding code, we have called `getAllUsers` and verified the total count. Let's test the single-user method in another test case:

```
// other methods
@Test
public void testSingleUser(){
    User user = userSevice.getUser(100);
    assertTrue(user.getUsername().contains("David"));
}
```

In the preceding code snippets, we just tested our service layer and verified the business logic. However, we can directly test the controller by using mocking methods, which will be discussed later in this chapter.

MockMvc

MockMvc is mainly used to test the code through the controller. By calling the controller (REST endpoint) directly, we can cover the whole application from MockMvc testing itself. Also, if we keep any authentication or restriction on the controller, it will also be covered in MockMvc test cases.

The following code will test our basic API (`localhost:8080/`) using MockMvc standards:

```
import static org.hamcrest.Matchers.is;
import static
org.springframework.test.web.servlet.result.MockMvcResultMatchers.jsonPath;
import static
org.springframework.test.web.servlet.result.MockMvcResultMatchers.status;
import org.junit.Before;
import org.junit.Test;
import org.junit.runner.RunWith;
import org.springframework.beans.factory.annotation.Autowired;
import org.springframework.boot.test.context.SpringBootTest;
import org.springframework.test.context.junit4.SpringJUnit4ClassRunner;
import org.springframework.test.web.servlet.MockMvc;
import org.springframework.test.web.servlet.MvcResult;
```

```
import org.springframework.test.web.servlet.request.MockMvcRequestBuilders;
import org.springframework.test.web.servlet.setup.MockMvcBuilders;
import org.springframework.web.context.WebApplicationContext;
@SpringBootTest
@RunWith(SpringJUnit4ClassRunner.class)
public class UserMockMVCTests {
  @Autowired
  private WebApplicationContext ctx;
  private MockMvc mockMvc;
  @Before
  public void setUp() {
    this.mockMvc = MockMvcBuilders.webAppContextSetup(this.ctx).build();
  }
  @Test
  public void testBasicMVC() throws Exception {
    MvcResult result = mockMvc
        .perform(MockMvcRequestBuilders.get("/"))
        .andExpect(status().isOk())
        .andExpect(jsonPath("result", is("Aloha")))
        .andReturn();
    String content = result.getResponse().getContentAsString();
     System.out.println("{testBasicMVC} response : " + content);
  }
}
```

In the preceding code, we only initialized the web application in the `setUp()` method. Also, we have bound `WebApplicationContext` by using the `@Autowired` annotation. Once the setup is ready, we create a method called `testBasicMVC` to test our plain API (`localhost:8080`), which will return `"result: Aloha"`.

Once we have finished with the code, if we run it on Eclipse by selecting **Run As | JUnit test**, the preceding method will be executed and show the results. We can view the successful test case results in a JUnit window in Eclipse.

Testing a single user

So far, we have only tested a plain REST API. Here, we can go one step further and test our user API by getting a single user from `userid`. The following code will take us through the implementation of getting a single user:

```
import static org.hamcrest.Matchers.is;
import static org.springframework.test.web.servlet.result.MockMvcResultMatchers.jsonPath;
import static
```

```java
      org.springframework.test.web.servlet.result.MockMvcResultMatchers.status;
import org.junit.Before;
import org.junit.Test;
import org.junit.runner.RunWith;
import org.springframework.beans.factory.annotation.Autowired;
import org.springframework.boot.test.context.SpringBootTest;
import org.springframework.test.context.junit4.SpringJUnit4ClassRunner;
import org.springframework.test.web.servlet.MockMvc;
import org.springframework.test.web.servlet.MvcResult;
import org.springframework.test.web.servlet.request.MockMvcRequestBuilders;
import org.springframework.test.web.servlet.setup.MockMvcBuilders;
import org.springframework.web.context.WebApplicationContext;
@SpringBootTest
@RunWith(SpringJUnit4ClassRunner.class)
public class UserMockMVCTests {
  @Autowired
  private WebApplicationContext ctx;
  private MockMvc mockMvc;
  @Before
  public void setUp() {
    this.mockMvc = MockMvcBuilders.webAppContextSetup(this.ctx).build();
  }
  @Test
  public void testBasicMVC() throws Exception {
    MvcResult result = mockMvc
        .perform(MockMvcRequestBuilders.get("/"))
        .andExpect(status().isOk())
        .andExpect(jsonPath("result", is("Aloha")))
        .andReturn();
    String content = result.getResponse().getContentAsString();
     System.out.println("{testBasicMVC} response : " + content);
  }
  @Test
  public void testSingleUser() throws Exception {
    MvcResult result = mockMvc
        .perform(MockMvcRequestBuilders.get("/user/100"))
        .andExpect(status().isOk())
        .andExpect(jsonPath("userid", is(100)))
        .andExpect(jsonPath("username", is("David")))
        .andReturn();
    String content = result.getResponse().getContentAsString();
    System.out.println("{testSingleUser} response : " + content);
  }
}
```

In the preceding code (`testSingleUser`), we can see that we are expecting `status`, `userid`, and `username` as `Ok`, `100`, and `David`, respectively. Also, we print the result that we get from the REST API.

Postman

We have already used Postman in previous chapters for testing our REST APIs. Postman will be helpful when we need to test the application completely. In Postman, we can write test suites to validate our REST API endpoints.

Getting all the users – Postman

First, we shall start with a simple API for getting all the users:

```
http://localhost:8080/user
```

The earlier method will get all the users. The Postman screenshot for getting all the users is as follows:

Testing RESTful Web Services

In the preceding screenshot, we can see that we get all the users that we added before. We have used the GET method to call this API.

Adding a user – Postman

Let's try to use the POST method in user to add a new user:

```
http://localhost:8080/user
```

Add the user, as shown in the following screenshot:

In the preceding result, we can see the JSON output:

```
{
    "result" : "added"
}
```

Generating a JWT – Postman

Let's try generating the token (JWT) by calling the generate token API in Postman using the following code:

```
http://localhost:8080/security/generate/token
```

We can clearly see that we use `subject` in the **Body** to generate the token. Once we call the API, we will get the token. We can check the token in the following screenshot:

Getting the subject from the token

By using our existing token that we created before, we will get the subject by calling the get subject API:

```
http://localhost:8080/security/get/subject
```

The result will be as shown in the following screenshot:

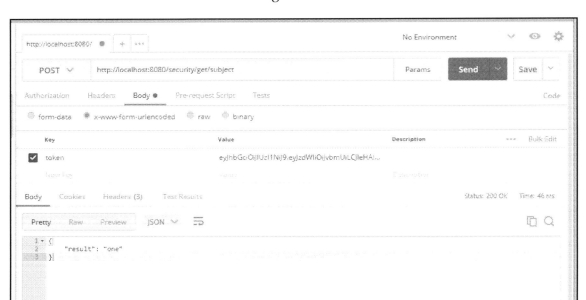

In the preceding API call, we sent the token in the API to get the subject. We can see the subject in the resulting JSON.

SoapUI

Like Postman, SoapUI is another open source tool that is used to test web services. SoapUI helps in web service invoking, mocking, simulation, load testing, and functional testing. SoapUI is heavily used in load testing, and it has lots of controls to make load testing easy.

SoapUI is very easy to install in operating systems such as Windows and Linux. Its user interface gives us a lot of flexibility to build complex test scenarios. Also, SoapUI supports third-party plugins such as `TestMaker` and `Agiletestware`, and it's easy to integrate with IDEs such as NetBeans and Eclipse.

Getting all the users – SoapUI

We will use SoapUI to test our basic API (/user). The following method will get all the users when we use them in SoapUI using the GET method:

```
http://localhost:8080/user
```

The SoapUI screenshot for getting all the users is as follows:

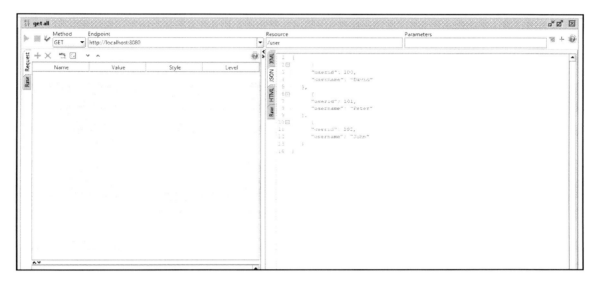

We will try to add a user using the POST method:

```
http://localhost:8080/user
```

Testing RESTful Web Services

The added user screenshot will be as follows:

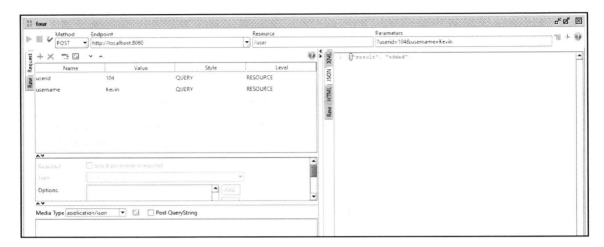

In this result, we can see the JSON output:

```
{"result" : "added"}
```

Generating JWT SoapUI

We will generate the token using the `GET` method as follows:

```
http://localhost:8080/security/generate/token
```

In SoapUI, we are using `subject` as a parameter. We can see this in the following screenshot:

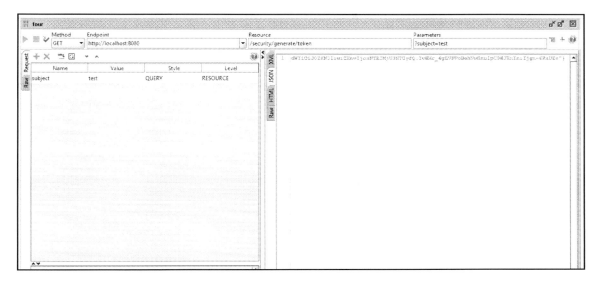

We can clearly see that we use `subject` in the body to generate the token. Also, we can see the **Style** as **QUERY** in SoapUI. This will make our **Value** (`test`) as a parameter for the API.

Once we call the API, we will get the token. We can check the token in the preceding screenshot.

Getting the subject from the token – SoapUI

Now we can get the subject from the token generated previously. We may need to pass the token as a parameter to get the subject.

The following API will get the subject from the token when we call the API in SoapUI using the `GET` method:

```
http://localhost:8080/security/get/subject
```

Although we can use the `POST` method in the preceding API call, we only used the `GET` method to simplify the process, as shown in the following screenshot:

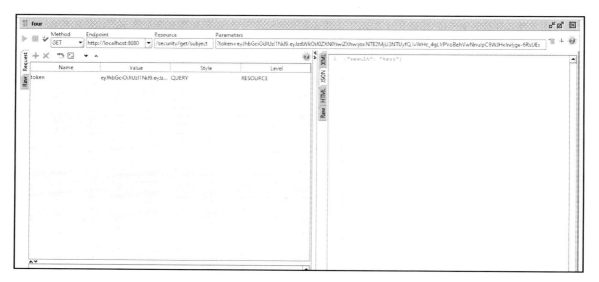

In the preceding API call, we sent the token in the API to get the subject. We can see the subject in the resulting JSON.

So far, we have tested our APIs with the help of SoapUI. Although SoapUI seems a little tougher than Postman, it might be very helpful when we do load testing and security testing at the enterprise level.

jsoup

jsoup is a Java library for extracting HTML documents and getting the details from HTML DOM. jsoup uses DOM, CSS, and jQuery-like methods to retrieve information from any web page. Even though jsoup is mainly used for HTML document parsing, in our application we will use it for API testing.

First, we will call the REST API in jsoup and convert the result to JSON. To convert strings to JSON we will use the Gson library.

For both jsoup and Gson libraries, we may have to add dependencies in our `pom.xml`. The following is the code for both jsoup and Gson dependencies:

```xml
<dependency>
   <groupId>org.jsoup</groupId>
   <artifactId>jsoup</artifactId>
   <version>1.8.2</version>
</dependency>
<dependency>
    <groupId>com.google.code.gson</groupId>
    <artifactId>gson</artifactId>
    <version>2.8.2</version>
</dependency>
```

We will use the jsoup REST consumer inside the test resources so it will be easier to test:

```
String doc = Jsoup.connect("http://localhost:8080/user").ignoreContentType(true).get().body().text();
```

The following code will call the REST API as HTML and get the body as text. By doing this, we will get only the REST API results as JSON text. The JSON text is as follows:

```
[{"userid":100,"username":"David"},{"userid":101,"username":"Peter"},{"userid":102,"username":"John"}]
```

Once we get the JSON text, we can convert them into a JSON array by using the `JsonParser` class. The following code will parse the JSON text and convert it into the `JsonArray` class:

```
JsonParser parser = new JsonParser();
JsonElement userElement = parser.parse(doc);
JsonArray userArray = userElement.getAsJsonArray();
```

Once we get the JSON array, we can simply check the array size to verify our REST API. The following code will test the size of our REST API:

```
assertEquals(3, userArray.size());
```

Here is the complete class with the preceding code mentioned:

```
import static org.junit.Assert.assertEquals;
import java.io.IOException;
import org.jsoup.Jsoup;
```

```
import org.junit.Test;
import org.junit.runner.RunWith;
import org.slf4j.Logger;
import org.slf4j.LoggerFactory;
import org.springframework.boot.test.context.SpringBootTest;
import org.springframework.test.context.junit4.SpringRunner;
import com.google.gson.Gson;
import com.google.gson.JsonArray;
import com.google.gson.JsonElement;
import com.google.gson.JsonParser;
import com.packtpub.model.User;
@RunWith(SpringRunner.class)
@SpringBootTest
public class JsoupUserTest {
   private final Logger _log = LoggerFactory.getLogger(this.getClass());
   @Test
   public void testUsersJsoup() throws IOException{
      String doc =
Jsoup.connect("http://localhost:8080/user").ignoreContentType(true).get().body().text();
      _log.info("{test} doc : "+doc);
      JsonParser parser = new JsonParser();
      JsonElement userElement = parser.parse(doc);
      JsonArray userArray = userElement.getAsJsonArray();
      _log.info("{test} size : "+userArray.size());
      assertEquals(3, userArray.size());
   }
}
```

In the preceding method, we have used loggers to print the size. Also, we have used the assertEquals method to check the user array size.

As this is like a JUnit test, we may need to test with the JUnit Test option in Eclipse. We can simply right-click the file and click **Run As | JUnit Test**.

Getting a user – jsoup

In the earlier method, we have tested get all users in the REST API. Now, we can check a single user and details. The following code will test the single user REST API:

```
@Test
public void testUserJsoup() throws IOException{
   String doc =
Jsoup.connect("http://localhost:8080/user/100").ignoreContentType(true).get().body().text();
```

```
        Gson g = new Gson();
        User user = g.fromJson(doc, User.class);
        assertEquals("David", user.getUsername());
    }
```

The preceding code will call the REST API, get the JSON in text format, and then convert them into a User class. Once we convert them into the User class, we can check the username by assertEquals.

Adding a user – jsoup

Let's try to use the POST method in jsoup by adding a new user. In this REST API (add user), we may need to pass a few parameters to the REST API. The following code will call the add user API and get the results:

```
@Autowired
UserService userSevice;
@Test
public void testUserAdditionJsoup() throws IOException{
    String doc = Jsoup.connect("http://localhost:8080/user/")
        .data("userid", "103")
        .data("username", "kevin")
        .ignoreContentType(true)
        .post().body().text();
    Gson g = new Gson();
    Map<String, Object> result = g.fromJson(doc, Map.class);
    _log.info("{test} result : "+result);
    assertEquals("added", result.get("result"));
    // user should be deleted as we tested the case already
    userSevice.deleteUser(103);
}
```

In the preceding code, we have used the .post() method to call the API. Also, we have used the .data() method to pass the parameters. By adding .ignoreContentType() we tell the Jsoup library that we don't care about the content type that the API returns. Also, body().text() will get the body as a text.

By checking the result in assertEquals, we make sure that the API works fine.

To test jsoup, the server needs to be running, so we need to run the server first. Then we can run our test cases. To run other test cases, such as JUnit and MockMvc, we don't need the server.

Running the test cases

First, we run the server and make sure we can access the server. If we don't run the server, we will not be able to test jsoup, so keep the server running. Once the server has started, right-click the project **Run As** | **JUnit Test**. We can see the results in the JUnit window, as shown in the following screenshot:

In the preceding screenshot, we can clearly see that all of our test cases have passed.

Summary

In this chapter, we discussed various testing methods for RESTful web services. We have applied JUnit testing, MockMvc, Postman, and SoapUI. These testing methods will be very helpful for testing the business logic in the application. In the next chapter, we will talk about the REST client and consuming RESTful services in a REST client.

8
Performance

Performance is considered a primary criterion when it comes to RESTful web services in an application. This chapter will focus mainly on how we can improve the performance in our application and reduce the response time. Though performance optimization techniques can be applied in different layers of web applications, we will talk about the RESTful (web) layer. The remaining performance optimization techniques will be discussed in `Chapter 11`, *Scaling*.

The following topics will be discussed in this chapter:

- HTTP compression
- HTTP caching and HTTP cache control
- Cache implementation in the REST API
- Using HTTP If-Modified-Since headers and ETags

HTTP compression

In order to get content quickly from a REST service, data can be compressed and sent over protocols such as HTTP. While compressing data, we will have to follow some encoding format, so the same format will be applied on the receiver side.

Content negotiation

While requesting a resource in the server, the client will have many options to receive the content in various representations. For example, DOC/PDF is the data type representation. Turkish or English is the language representation, where the server can send the resource in a particular language. There must be some agreement between the server and the client about which format the resource will be accessed in, such as language, data type, and so on. The process is called **content negotiation**.

Here, we will talk about two different content negotiation mechanisms: server-driven and agent-driven mechanisms. Before moving on to these mechanisms, we will talk about Accept-Encoding and Content-Encoding, as they are important.

Accept-Encoding

The client will tell the server about which compression algorithm(s) it can receive. The most common types of encoding are `gzip` and `deflate`. While requesting the server, the client will share encoding types in the request headers. Accept-Encoding will be used for such purposes. Simply put, the client will say, "I will accept only the mentioned compression formats" to the server.

We will see sample `Accept-Encoding` as follows:

```
Accept-Encoding: gzip, deflate
```

In the preceding header, the client says that it can accept only `gzip` or `deflate` in the response.

Other possible options are mentioned as follows:

```
Accept-Encoding: compress, gzip
Accept-Encoding:
Accept-Encoding: *
Accept-Encoding: compress;q=0.5, gzip;q=1.0
Accept-Encoding: gzip;q=1.0, identity; q=0.5, *;q=0
```

We can see the `compress` value followed by `q=0.5`, which means the quality rating is only `0.5` when compared to the `gzip` rating of `q=1.0`, which is very high. In this case, the client is recommending the server that it can get `gzip` over `compress`. However, if `gzip` is not possible, `compress` is fine for the client.

If the server doesn't support the compression algorithm that the client requested, the server should send an error response with the `406 (Not Acceptable)` status code.

Content-Encoding

Content-Encoding is an entity header that is used to compress the data type to be sent to the client from the server. The Content-Encoding value tells the client which encodings were used in the entity-body. It will tell the client how to decode the data to retrieve the value.

Let's have a look at the single and multiple encoding options:

```
// Single Encoding option
Content-Encoding: gzip
Content-Encoding: compress

// Multiple Encoding options
Content-Encoding: gzip, identity
Content-Encoding: deflate, gzip
```

In the preceding configuration, single and multiple options are provided on Content-Encoding. Here, the server tells the client that it can offer `gzip` and `compress` algorithm-based encoding. If the multiple encoding is mentioned by the server, those encodings will be applied in the mentioned order.

Compressing data as much as possible is highly recommended.

Changing Content-Encoding on-the-fly is not recommended. As it will collapse future requests (such as PUT on GET), changing Content-Encoding on the fly is not a good idea at all.

Server-driven content negotiation

Server-driven content negotiation is performed by server-side algorithms to decide on the best representation that the server has to send to the client. It's also called proactive content negotiation. In server-driven negotiation, the client (user-agent) will give options of various representations with quality ratings. Algorithms in the server will have to decide which representation would work best for client-provided criteria.

For example, the client requests a resource by sharing the media type criterion, with ratings such as which media type would be better for the client. The server will do the rest of the work and supply the best representation of the resource that suits the client's needs.

Agent-driven content negotiation

Agent-driven content negotiation is performed by algorithms on the client side. When the client requests a particular resource, the server will tell the client about various representations of the resource, with metadata such as content type, quality, and so on. Then the client side algorithms will decide which will be the best and request it from the server again. This is also called reactive content negotiation.

HTTP caching

When the client requests the same resource representation many times, it will be a waste of time to provide it from the server side and it will be time-consuming in web applications. Instead of talking to the server, if the the resource is reused it will definitely improve the web application performance.

Caching will be considered a primary option for bringing performance to our web application. Web caches avoid server contact multiple times and reduce the latency; hence, the application will be faster. Caching can be applied on different layers of an application. In this chapter, we will only talk about HTTP caching, which is considered a middle layer. We will dig more into other forms of caching in Chapter 11, *Scaling*.

HTTP cache control

Cache control is a header field that specifies directives for caching operations on the web. These directives give the caching authorization, define the duration of the caching, and so on. The directives define the behavior, usually intended to prevent caching responses.

Here, we will talk about HTTP caching directives: the `public`, `private`, `no-cache`, and `only-if-cached` directives.

Public caching

If the cache control allows public caching, the resource can be cached by multiple user cache. We can do this by setting the `public` option in the `Cache-Control` header. In public caching, the response may be cached by multiple user cache, even the non-cacheable or cacheable, only within a non-share cache:

```
Cache-Control: public
```

In the preceding setting, `public` indicates that the response can be cached by any cache.

Private caching

Unlike public caching, private responses are applicable for a single user cache, not for a shared cache. In private caching, intermediates can't cache the content:

```
Cache-Control: private
```

The preceding setting indicates that the response is available for a single user only, and it should not be accessed by any other caches.

Also, we can specify how long the content should be cached in our heading settings. This can be done by the `max-age` directive option.

Check the following setting:

```
Cache-Control: private, max-age=600
```

In the preceding setting, we mentioned that the response can be cached in private mode (single user only) and the maximum amount of time the resource will be considered fresh.

No-cache

Caching might not be needed for accessing dynamic resources. In such situations, we can use a `no-cache` setting in our cache control to avoid client-side caching:

```
Cache-Control: no-cache
```

The preceding setting will tell the client to check the server whenever the resource is being requested.

Also, in some situations, we may need to disable the caching mechanism itself. This can be done using `no-store` in our setting:

```
Cache-Control: no-store
```

The preceding setting will tell the client to avoid resource caching and get the resource from the server always.

HTTP/1.0 caches will not follow the no-cache directive, as it was introduced in HTTP/1.1

Cache control was introduced only in HTTP/1.1. In HTTP /1.0, only **Pragma: no-cache** is used to prevent responses being cached.

Only-if-cached

In some scenarios, like poor network connectivity, a client might want to return the cached resource and not reload or revalidate with the server. To achieve this, the client can include the `only-if-cached` directive in the request. If it is received, the client will get the cached entry, or else respond with a 504 (gateway timeout) status.

These cache control directives can override the default caching algorithms.

So far, we have discussed various cache control directives and their explanations. The following are sample settings for both cache requests and cache response directives.

Request cache control directives (standard `Cache-Control` directives, which can be used by the client in an HTTP request) are as follows:

```
Cache-Control: max-age=<seconds>
Cache-Control: max-stale[=<seconds>]
Cache-Control: min-fresh=<seconds>
Cache-Control: no-cache
Cache-Control: no-store
Cache-Control: no-transform
Cache-Control: only-if-cached
```

Response cache control directives (standard `Cache-Control` directives, which can be used by the server in an HTTP response) are as follows:

```
Cache-Control: must-revalidate
Cache-Control: no-cache
Cache-Control: no-store
Cache-Control: no-transform
Cache-Control: public
Cache-Control: private
Cache-Control: proxy-revalidate
Cache-Control: max-age=<seconds>
Cache-Control: s-maxage=<seconds>
```

It is not possible to specify cache directives for a specific cache.

Cache validation

When a cache has a fresh entry that can be used as a response when the client requests, it will check with the originating server to see if the cached entry is still usable. This process is called **cache validation**. Also, revalidation is triggered when the user presses the reload button. If the cached response includes the `Cache-Control: must revalidate` header, it will be triggered under normal browsing.

When the resource's time is expired, it will either be validated or fetched again. Cache validation will only be triggered when the server provided a strong or weak validator.

ETags

ETags provide a mechanism for validating cached responses. The ETag response header can be used as a strong validator. In this case, the client can neither understand the value nor predict what its value will be. When the server issues a response, it generates a token that hides the state of the resource:

```
ETag : ijk564
```

If the `ETag` is part of the response, the client can issue an `If-None-Match` in the header of the future request to validate the cached resource:

```
If-None-Match: ijk564
```

The server will compare the requested header with the current state of the resource. If the resource state is changed, the server will respond with a new resource. Otherwise, the server will return a `304 Not Modified` response.

Last-Modified/If-Modified-Since headers

So far, we have seen a strong validator (ETags). Here, we will discuss a weak validator that can be used in the header. The `Last-Modified` response header can be used as a weak validator. Instead of generating a hash of a resource, a timestamp will be used to check the cached responses are valid.

As this validator has a 1-second resolution, it is considered weak compared to ETags. If the Last-Modified header is present in a response, then the client can send an If-Modified-Since request header to validate the cached resource.

The If-Modified-Since header is supplied from the client when requesting a resource. To simplify the mechanism in a real example, the client request would resemble this: "I have already cached the resource XYZ at 10 A.M.; however, get the updated XYZ if it's changed since 10 A.M. otherwise just return 304. Then I will use the previously cached XYZ."

Cache implementation

So far, we have seen the theory part in this chapter. Let's try to implement the concept in our application. To simplify the cache implementation, we are going to use only user management. We will use the getUser (single user) REST API to apply our caching concept.

The REST resource

In the getUser method, we will pass the right userid to the path variable, assuming the client will pass the userid and get the resource. There are many caching options available to implement. Here, we will use only the If-Modified-Since caching mechanism. As this mechanism will pass the If-Modified-Since value in the header, it will be forwarded to the server, saying that, if the resource is changed after the specified time, get the resource fresh, or else return null.

There are many ways we can implement caching. As our goal is to simplify and convey the message clearly, we will keep the code simple, instead of adding complexity in the code. In order to implement this caching, we might need to add a new variable called updatedDate in our User class. Let's add the variable in our class.

The updatedDate variable will be used as a checking variable for If-Modified-Since caching, as we will rely on user-updated date.

The client will ask the server if the user data has changed since the last cached time. The server will check against the user updatedDate and return null if not updated; otherwise, or else it will return fresh data:

```
private Date updatedDate;
public Date getUpdatedDate() {
  return updatedDate;
```

```
    }
    public void setUpdatedDate(Date updatedDate) {
       this.updatedDate = updatedDate;
    }
```

In the preceding code, we have just added a new variable, `updatedDate`, and added the proper getter and setter methods into it. We might clean up these getter and setter methods later by adding the Lombok library. We will apply Lombok in upcoming chapters.

Also, we need to add another constructor to initialize the `updatedDate` variable when we get the instance of the class. Let's add the constructor here:

```
    public User(Integer userid, String username, Date updatedDate){
       this.userid = userid;
       this.username = username;
       this.updatedDate = updatedDate;
    }
```

If possible, we can change the `toString` method as follows:

```
    @Override
    public String toString() {
       return "User [userid=" + userid + ", username=" + username + ", updatedDate=" + updatedDate + "]";
    }
```

After adding all the preceding details mentioned, our class will look as follows:

```
package com.packtpub.model;
import java.io.Serializable;
import java.util.Date;
public class User implements Serializable {
   private static final long serialVersionUID = 1L;
   public User() {
   }
   private Integer userid;
   private String username;
   private Date updatedDate;
   public User(Integer userid, String username) {
      this.userid = userid;
      this.username = username;
   }
   public User(Integer userid, String username, Date updatedDate) {
      this.userid = userid;
      this.username = username;
      this.updatedDate = updatedDate;
   }
```

Performance

```java
    public Date getUpdatedDate() {
      return updatedDate;
    }
    public void setUpdatedDate(Date updatedDate) {
      this.updatedDate = updatedDate;
    }
    public Integer getUserid() {
      return userid;
    }
    public void setUserid(Integer userid) {
      this.userid = userid;
    }
    public String getUsername() {
      return username;
    }
    public void setUsername(String username) {
      this.username = username;
    }
    @Override
    public String toString() {
      return "User [userid=" + userid + ", username=" + username + ", updatedDate=" + updatedDate + "]";
    }
}
```

Now, we will go back to `UserController`, which we introduced in previous chapters, and change the `getUser` method:

```java
@RestController
@RequestMapping("/user")
public class UserController {
    // other methods and variables (hidden)
    @ResponseBody
    @RequestMapping("/{id}")
    public User getUser(@PathVariable("id") Integer id, WebRequest webRequest){
        User user = userSevice.getUser(id);
        long updated = user.getUpdatedDate().getTime();
        boolean isNotModified = webRequest.checkNotModified(updated);
        logger.info("{getUser} isNotModified : "+isNotModified);
        if(isNotModified){
           logger.info("{getUser} resource not modified since last call, so exiting");
           return null;
        }
        logger.info("{getUser} resource modified since last call, so get the updated content");
```

```
            return userSevice.getUser(id);
    }
}
```

In the preceding code, we used the `WebRequest` parameter in our existing method. The `WebRequest` object will be used for calling the `checkNotModified` method. At first, we get the user details by `id` and get the `updatedDate` in milliseconds. We check the user updated date against the client header information (we assume the client will pass `If-Not-Modified-Since` in the header). If the user-updated date is newer than the cached date, we assume the user is updated, so we will have to send the new resource.

 We might have to import `org.apache.log4j.Logger` since we added the logger in `UserController`. Otherwise it will show error while compiling.

If the user is not updated after the cached (by the client) date, it will simply return null. Also, we have provided enough loggers to print our desired statements.

Let's test the REST API in SoapUI or the Postman client. When we call the API the first time, it will return the data with header information, as follows:

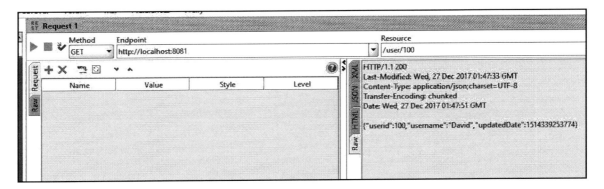

SoapUI client

We can see that we are using the GET method for this API and the response header on the right side.

[119]

Performance

> In our preceding screenshot we have used the port 8081. By default Spring Boot works on port 8080. If you want to change it to 8081, configure the port in /src/main/resources/application.properties as follows:
>
> server.port = 8081
>
> If there is not application.properties under the mentioned location, you can create one.

The response (JSON) looks as follows:

```
{
    "userid": 100,
    "username": "David",
    "updatedDate": 1516201175654
}
```

In the preceding JSON response, we can see the user details, including updatedDate.

The response (header) is as follows:

```
HTTP/1.1 200
Last-Modified: Wed, 17 Jan 2018 14:59:35 GMT
ETag: "06acb280fd1c0435ac4ddcc6de0aeeee7"
Content-Type: application/json;charset=UTF-8
Content-Length: 61
Date: Wed, 17 Jan 2018 14:59:59 GMT

{"userid":100,"username":"David","updatedDate":1516201175654}
```

In the preceding response header, we can see the HTTP result 200 (meaning OK) and the Last-Modified date.

Now, we will add If-Modified-Since in the headers and update the latest date we got from the previous response. We can check the If-Modified-Since parameter in the following screenshot:

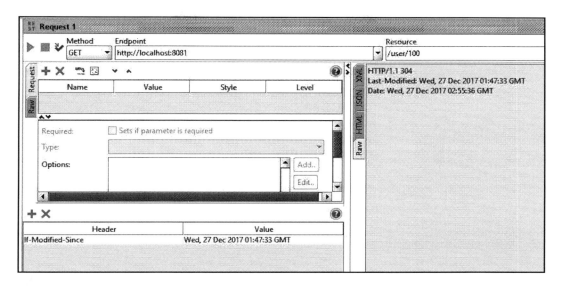

In the preceding configuration, we have added the If-Modified-Since parameter in the header section and called the same REST API again. The code will check whether the resource has been updated since the last cached date. In our case, the resource is not updated, so it will simply return 304 in the response. We can see the response as follows:

```
HTTP/1.1 304
Last-Modified: Wed, 17 Jan 2018 14:59:35 GMT
Date: Wed, 17 Jan 2018 15:05:29 GMT
```

The HTTP 304 (not modified) response simply conveys to the client that there is no resource modified, so the client can use the existing cache.

If we update the specified user by calling the update REST API (http://localhost:8081/user/100 using PUT) and then call the previous API (http://localhost:8081/user/100 using GET), we will get a fresh resource as the user is updated after the client cache.

Caching with ETags

In the previous section, we explored caching based on the updated date. However, we may not always need to rely on the updated date when we need to check the updated resource. There is another mechanism, called ETag caching, that provides a strong validator to check whether the resource is updated or not. ETag caching would be the perfect alternative for regular caching by checking the updated date.

Performance

In ETag caching, the response header will provide the hashed ID (MD5) for the body. If the resource is updated, the header will generate a new hash ID on the REST API call. So we don't need to explicitly check the information like we did in the previous section.

Spring provides a filter called `ShallowEtagHeaderFilter` to support ETag caching. Let's try to add the `ShallowEtagHeaderFilter` in our existing application. We will add the code in our main application file (`TicketManagementApplication`):

```
@Bean
public Filter shallowEtagHeaderFilter() {
   return new ShallowEtagHeaderFilter();
}
@Bean
public FilterRegistrationBean shallowEtagHeaderFilterRegistration() {
   FilterRegistrationBean result = new FilterRegistrationBean();
   result.setFilter(this.shallowEtagHeaderFilter());
   result.addUrlPatterns("/user/*");
   result.setName("shallowEtagHeaderFilter");
   result.setOrder(1);
   return result;
}
```

In the preceding code, we are adding `ShallowEtagHeaderFilter` as a bean and registering by supplying our URL patterns and name. As we will test only the user resource at the moment, we will add `/user/*` in our patterns. Finally, our main application class will look as follows:

```
package com.packtpub.restapp.ticketmanagement;
import javax.servlet.Filter;
import org.springframework.boot.SpringApplication;
import org.springframework.boot.autoconfigure.SpringBootApplication;
import org.springframework.boot.web.servlet.FilterRegistrationBean;
import org.springframework.context.annotation.Bean;
import org.springframework.context.annotation.ComponentScan;
import org.springframework.context.annotation.ImportResource;
import org.springframework.web.filter.ShallowEtagHeaderFilter;
@ComponentScan("com.packtpub")
@SpringBootApplication
public class TicketManagementApplication {
   public static void main(String[] args) {
      SpringApplication.run(TicketManagementApplication.class, args);
   }
   @Bean
   public Filter shallowEtagHeaderFilter() {
      return new ShallowEtagHeaderFilter();
   }
```

```
@Bean
public FilterRegistrationBean shallowEtagHeaderFilterRegistration() {
   FilterRegistrationBean result = new FilterRegistrationBean();
   result.setFilter(this.shallowEtagHeaderFilter());
   result.addUrlPatterns("/user/*");
   result.setName("shallowEtagHeaderFilter");
   result.setOrder(1);
   return result;
  }
}
```

We can test this ETag mechanism by calling the user API (http://localhost:8081/user). When we call this API, the server will return the following headers:

```
HTTP/1.1 200
ETag: "02a4bc8613aefc333de37c72bfd5e392a"
Content-Type: application/json;charset=UTF-8
Content-Length: 186
Date: Wed, 17 Jan 2018 15:11:45 GMT
```

We can see that ETag is added in our header with the hash ID. Now we will call the same API with the If-None-Match header with the hash value. We will see the header in the following screenshot:

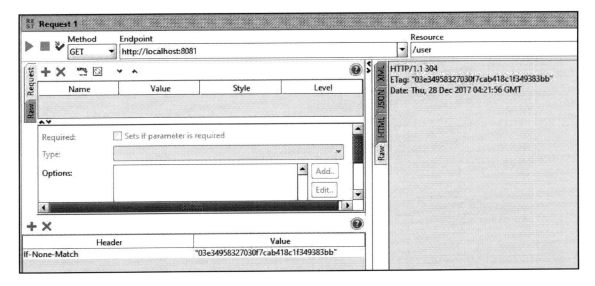

When we call the same API again with the `If-None-Match` header and the value of our previously hashed ID, the server will return a `304` state, which we can see as follows:

```
HTTP/1.1 304
ETag: "02a4bc8613aefc333de37c72bfd5e392a"
Date: Wed, 17 Jan 2018 15:12:24 GMT
```

In this mechanism, the actual response body will not be sent to the client. Instead, it will tell the client that the resource is not modified, so the client can use the previously cached content. The `304` state conveys that the resource is not cached.

Summary

In this chapter, we have learned HTTP optimization methods to improve application performance. By reducing the interaction between clients and servers and the size of the data over HTTP, we will achieve maximum performance in our REST API services. We will explore other optimization, caching, and scaling techniques in `Chapter 11`, *Scaling*, as we will be talking about more advanced topics relating to web service performance.

9
AOP and Logger Controls

In this chapter, we will learn about Spring **Aspect-Oriented Programming** (**AOP**) and logger controls, both their theory and implementation. We will integrate Spring AOP in our existing REST APIs and walk through how AOP and logger controls will make our lives easier.

In this chapter, we will cover the following topics:

- Spring AOP theory
- Implementation of Spring AOP
- Why do we need logger controls?
- How do we implement logger controls?
- Integrating Spring AOP and logger controls

Aspect-oriented programming (AOP)

Aspect-oriented programming is a concept where we add a new behavior to existing code without modifying the code itself. The AOP concept is really helpful when it comes to logging or method authentication.

There are many ways you can use AOP in Spring. Let's not get into much detail, as it will be a big topic to discuss. Here, we will discuss only the `@Before` pointcut and how to use `@Before` in our business logic.

AOP (@Before) with execution

The term execution in AOP means having a pointcut in the `@Aspect` annotation itself, and it doesn't depend on the controller API. The alternate way is that you will have to explicitly mention the annotation in the API call. Let's talk about the explicit pointcut in the next topic:

```
package com.packtpub.aop;
import org.aspectj.lang.annotation.Aspect;
import org.aspectj.lang.annotation.Before;
import org.springframework.stereotype.Component;
@Aspect
@Component
public class TokenRequiredAspect {
  @Before("execution(* com.packtpub.restapp.HomeController.testAOPExecution())")
  public void tokenRequiredWithoutAnnoation() throws Throwable{
    System.out.println("Before tokenRequiredWithExecution");
  }
}
```

In this pointcut, we have used the `@Before` annotation, and it uses `execution(* com.packtpub.restapp.HomeController.testAOPWithoutAnnotation())`, which means this pointcut will be focusing on a specific method, the `testAOPWithoutAnnotation` method inside the `HomeController` class, in our case.

For AOP-related work, we might need to add the dependency to our `pom.xml` file, which is mentioned as follows:

```
<dependency>
    <groupId>org.aspectj</groupId>
    <artifactId>aspectjweaver</artifactId>
    <version>1.8.13</version>
</dependency>
```

The preceding dependency will bring all aspect-oriented classes to support our AOP implementation in this chapter.

@Aspect: This annotation is used to make the class support aspects. In Spring, aspects can be implemented using XML configurations or annotation, such as @Aspect.

@Component: This annotation will make the class scannable according to the rule of Spring's component scanner. By mentioning this class with @Component and @Aspect, we tell Spring to scan this class and identify it as an aspect.

The code for the HomeController class is given as follows:

```
@ResponseBody
@RequestMapping("/test/aop/with/execution")
public Map<String, Object> testAOPExecution(){
  Map<String, Object> map = new LinkedHashMap<>();
  map.put("result", "Aloha");
  return map;
}
```

Here, we simply create a new method to test our AOP. You may not need to create a new API to test our AOP. As long you provide the appropriate method name, it should be okay. To make it easier for the reader, we have created a new method called testAOPExecution in the HomeContoller class.

Testing AOP @Before execution

Just call the API (http://localhost:8080/test/aop/with/execution) in the browser or using any other REST client; then, you should see the following in the console:

Before tokenRequiredWithExecution

Even though this log doesn't really help our business logic, we will keep it for now to keep things easier for the reader to understand the flow. Once we learn about AOP and how it functions, we will integrate it into our business logic.

AOP (@Before) with annotation

So far, we have seen an execution-based AOP method that can be used for one or more methods. However, in some places, we may need to keep the implementation plain to increase visibility. This will help us use it wherever it is needed, and it is not tied to any method. We call it explicit annotation-based AOP.

AOP and Logger Controls

In order to use this AOP concept, we may need to create an interface that will help us with what we need to achieve.

`TokenRequired` is just a base interface for our `Aspect` class. It will be supplied to our `Aspect` class, which is mentioned as follows:

```
package com.packtpub.aop;
import java.lang.annotation.ElementType;
import java.lang.annotation.Retention;
import java.lang.annotation.RetentionPolicy;
import java.lang.annotation.Target;
@Retention(RetentionPolicy.RUNTIME)
@Target(ElementType.METHOD)
public @interface TokenRequired {
}
```

`@Retention`: A retention policy determines at what point the annotation should be discarded. In our case, `RetentionPolicy.RUNTIME` will be retained for the JVM through runtime.

Other retention policies are as listed:

SOURCE: It will be retained only with the source code, and it will discarded during compile time. Once the code is compiled, the annotation will be useless, so it won't be written in the bytecode.

CLASS: It will be retained till compile time and will be discarded during runtime.

`@Target`: This annotation is applicable for the class level and matches at runtime. The target annotation can be used to collect the target object.

The following `tokenRequiredWithAnnotation` method will implement the business logic for our aspect. To keep the logic simple, we have just provided `System.out.println(..)`. Later, we will add the main logic to the method:

```
@Aspect
@Component
public class TokenRequiredAspect {
  // old method (with execution)
  @Before("@annotation(tokenRequired)")
  public void tokenRequiredWithAnnotation(TokenRequired tokenRequired)
throws Throwable{
    System.out.println("Before tokenRequiredWithAnnotation");
```

        }
    }

In the preceding code, we have created a method called `tokenRequiredWithAnnotation` and supplied the `TokenRequired` interface as a parameter for this method. We can see the annotation called `@Before` on top of this method with `@annotation(tokenRequired)`. This method will be called every time the `@TokenRequired` annotation is used in any method. You can see the annotation usage as follows:

```
@ResponseBody
@RequestMapping("/test/aop/with/annotation")
@TokenRequired
public Map<String, Object> testAOPAnnotation(){
  Map<String, Object> map = new LinkedHashMap<>();
  map.put("result", "Aloha");
  return map;
}
```

The main difference between the previous AOP method and this is `@TokenRequired`. In the old API caller, we didn't mention any AOP annotation explicitly, but we have to mention `@TokenRequired` in this caller as it will call the appropriate AOP method. Also, in this AOP method, we don't need to mention `execution`, like we did in the previous `execution(* com.packtpub.restapp.HomeController.testAOPWithoutAnnotation())` method.

Testing AOP @Before annotation

Just call the API (`http://localhost:8080/test/aop/with/annotation`) in the browser or using any other REST client; then, you should see the following on the console:

```
Before tokenRequiredWithAnnotation
```

Integrating AOP with JWT

Let's assume that you want to restrict the `deleteUser` option in the `UserContoller` method. Whoever deletes the user should have the proper JWT token. If they don't have the token with them, we won't let them delete any users. Here, we will first have a `packt` subject to create a token.

The `http://localhost:8080/security/generate/token?subject=packt`-generated token API can be called to generate the token.

[129]

AOP and Logger Controls

When we use `packt` in the subject, it will generate the eyJhbGciOiJIUzI1NiJ9.eyJzdWIiOiJwYWNrdCIsImV4cCI6MTUwOTk0NzY2Mn0.hIsVgg bam0pRoLOnSe8L9GQS4IFfFklborwJVthsmz0 **token**.

Now, we will have to create an AOP method to restrict the user by asking them to have the token in the header of the `delete` call:

```
@Before("@annotation(tokenRequired)")
public void tokenRequiredWithAnnotation(TokenRequired tokenRequired) throws Throwable{
        ServletRequestAttributes reqAttributes = 
(ServletRequestAttributes)RequestContextHolder.currentRequestAttributes();
        HttpServletRequest request = reqAttributes.getRequest();
        // checks for token in request header
        String tokenInHeader = request.getHeader("token");
        if(StringUtils.isEmpty(tokenInHeader)){
            throw new IllegalArgumentException("Empty token");
        }
        Claims claims = Jwts.parser()
.setSigningKey(DatatypeConverter.parseBase64Binary(SecurityServiceImpl.secretKey))
        .parseClaimsJws(tokenInHeader).getBody();
        if(claims == null || claims.getSubject() == null){
            throw new IllegalArgumentException("Token Error : Claim is null");
        }
        if(!claims.getSubject().equalsIgnoreCase("packt")){
            throw new IllegalArgumentExceptionception("Subject doesn't match in the token");
        }
}
```

Looking at the preceding code, you can see the JWT integration in AOP. Yes, we have integrated the JWT token verification part with AOP. So hereafter, if someone calls the `@TokenRequired`-annotated API, it will first come to the AOP method and check for a token match. If the token is empty, not matched, or expired, we will get an error. All possible errors will be discussed as follows.

Now, we can start using the `@TokenRequired` annotation in our API call in the `UserController` class. So whenever this `deleteUser` method is called, it will go to JWT, checking pointcut before executing the API method itself. By doing this, we can assure that the `deleteUser` method will not be called without a token.

The code for the `UserController` class is given here:

```
@ResponseBody
@TokenRequired
@RequestMapping(value = "", method = RequestMethod.DELETE)
public Map<String, Object> deleteUser(
    @RequestParam(value="userid") Integer userid){
  Map<String, Object> map = new LinkedHashMap<>();
  userSevice.deleteUser(userid);
  map.put("result", "deleted");
  return map;
}
```

If the token is empty or null, it will throw the following error:

```
{
   "timestamp": 1509949209993,
   "status": 500,
   "error": "Internal Server Error",
   "exception": "java.lang.reflect.UndeclaredThrowableException",
   "message": "No message available",
   "path": "/user"
}
```

If the token is matched, it will show the result without throwing any error. You'll see the following result:

```
{
    "result": "deleted"
}
```

If we don't provide any token in the headers, it might throw the following error:

```
{
   "timestamp": 1509948248281,
   "status": 500,
   "error": "Internal Server Error",
   "exception": "java.lang.IllegalArgumentException",
   "message": "JWT String argument cannot be null or empty.",
   "path": "/user"
}
```

If the token is expired, you will get the following error:

```
{
   "timestamp": 1509947985415,
   "status": 500,
   "error": "Internal Server Error",
```

```
    "exception": "io.jsonwebtoken.ExpiredJwtException",
    "message": "JWT expired at 2017-11-06T00:54:22-0500. Current time:
2017-11-06T00:59:45-0500",
    "path": "/test/aop/with/annotation"
}
```

Logger controls

Logging will be helpful when we need to track the output of a specific process. It will help us verify the process or find the root cause of the error when things go wrong after deploying our application in the server. Without loggers, it will be difficult to track and figure out the problem if anything happens.

There are many logging frameworks we can use in our application; Log4j and Logback are the two major frameworks used in most applications.

SLF4J, Log4J, and Logback

SLF4j is an API to help us choose Log4j or Logback or any other JDK logging during deployment. SLF4j is just an abstraction layer that gives freedom to the user who uses our logging API. If someone wants to use JDK logging or Log4j in their implementation, SLF4j will help them plug in the desired framework during runtime.

If we create an end product that can't be used by someone as a library, we can implement Log4j or Logback directly. However, if we have a code that can be used as a library, it would be better to go with SLF4j, so the user can follow any logging they want.

Logback is a better alternative for Log4j and provides native support for SLF4j.

Logback framework

We mentioned earlier that Logback is more preferable than Log4j; here we will discuss how to implement the Logback logging framework.

There are three modules in Logback:

1. `logback-core`: Basic logging
2. `logback-classic`: Improved logging and SLF4j support
3. `logback-access`: Servlet container support

The `logback-core` module is the base for other two modules in the Log4j framework. The `logback-classic` module is an improved version of Log4j with more features. Also, the `logback-classic` module implements the SLF4j API natively. Due to this native support, we can switch to different logging frameworks such as **Java Util Logging** (**JUL**) and Log4j.

The `logback-access` module provides support to servlet containers such as Tomcat/Jetty, specifically to provide HTTP-access log facilities.

Logback dependency and configuration

In order to use Logback in our application, we need the `logback-classic` dependency. However, the `logback-classic` dependency is already available in the `spring-boot-starter` dependency. We can check this with dependency tree (`mvn dependency:tree`) in our project folder:

```
mvn dependency:tree
```

While checking dependency tree in the project folder, we will get the whole tree for all of our dependencies. The following is the section where we can see the `logback-classic` dependency under the `spring-boot-starter` dependency:

```
[INFO] | +- org.springframework.boot:spring-boot-
starter:jar:1.5.7.RELEASE:compile
[INFO] | +- org.springframework.boot:spring-boot:jar:1.5.7.RELEASE:compile
[INFO] | +- org.springframework.boot:spring-boot-
autoconfigure:jar:1.5.7.RELEASE:compile
[INFO] | +- org.springframework.boot:spring-boot-starter-
logging:jar:1.5.7.RELEASE:compile
[INFO] | | +- ch.qos.logback:logback-classic:jar:1.1.11:compile
[INFO] | | | \- ch.qos.logback:logback-core:jar:1.1.11:compile
[INFO] | | +- org.slf4j:jcl-over-slf4j:jar:1.7.25:compile
[INFO] | | +- org.slf4j:jul-to-slf4j:jar:1.7.25:compile
[INFO] | | \- org.slf4j:log4j-over-slf4j:jar:1.7.25:compile
[INFO] | \- org.yaml:snakeyaml:jar:1.17:runtime
[INFO] +- com.fasterxml.jackson.core:jackson-databind:jar:2
```

Since the necessary dependency files are already available, we don't need to add any dependencies for Logback framework implementation.

Logging levels

As SLF4j defined these logging levels, whoever implements SLF4j should adapt the logging levels of SFL4j. The logging levels are as follows:

- `TRACE`: Detailed comments that might not be used in all cases
- `DEBUG`: Useful comments for debugging purposes in production
- `INFO`: General comments that might be helpful during development
- `WARN`: Warning messages that might be helpful in specific scenarios such as deprecated methods
- `ERROR`: Severe error messages to be watched out for by the developer

Let's add the logging configuration to the `application.properties` file:

```
# spring framework logging
logging.level.org.springframework = ERROR

# local application logging
logging.level.com.packtpub.restapp = INFO
```

In the preceding configuration, we have used logging configuration for both Spring Framework and our application. According to our configuration, it will print `ERROR` for Spring Framework and `INFO` for our application.

Logback implementation in class

Let's add a `Logger` to the class; in our case, we can use `UserController`. We have to import `org.slf4j.Logger` and `org.slf4j.LoggerFactory`. We can check the following code:

```
private static final Logger _logger =
LoggerFactory.getLogger(HomeController.class);
```

In the preceding code, we introduced the `_logger` instance. We use the `UserController` class as a parameter for the `_logger` instance.

Now, we have to use the `_logger` instance to print the message we wanted. Here, we have used `_logger.info()` to print the message:

```
package com.packtpub.restapp;
import org.slf4j.Logger;
import org.slf4j.LoggerFactory;
// other imports
```

```
@RestController
@RequestMapping("/")
public class HomeController {
  private static final Logger _logger =
LoggerFactory.getLogger(HomeController.class);
  @Autowired
  SecurityService securityService;
  @ResponseBody
  @RequestMapping("")
  public Map<String, Object> test() {
    Map<String, Object> map = new LinkedHashMap<>();
    map.put("result", "Aloha");
    _logger.trace("{test} trace");
    _logger.debug("{test} debug");
    _logger.info("{test} info");
    _logger.warn("{test} warn ");
    _logger.error("{test} error");
    return map;
  }
}
```

In the preceding code, we have used various loggers to print messages. When you restart the server and call the http://localhost:8080 REST API, you will see the following output in the console:

```
2018-01-15 16:29:55.951 INFO 17812 --- [nio-8080-exec-1]
com.packtpub.restapp.HomeController : {test} info
2018-01-15 16:29:55.951 WARN 17812 --- [nio-8080-exec-1]
com.packtpub.restapp.HomeController : {test} warn
2018-01-15 16:29:55.951 ERROR 17812 --- [nio-8080-exec-1]
com.packtpub.restapp.HomeController : {test} error
```

As you can see from the log, the class name will always be in the log to identify the specific class in the log. As we haven't mentioned any logging pattern, the logger takes the default pattern to print the output with the class. If we need, we can change the pattern in our configuration file to get customized logging.

In the preceding code, we have used different logging levels to print the messages. There is a restriction on the logging level, so based on the business requirements and implementation, we will have to configure our logging levels.

In our logger configuration, we have used only the console printing option. We can also provide an option to print to external files wherever we want.

Summary

In this chapter, we covered Spring AOP and logger controls with implementation. In our existing code, we introduced Spring AOP and walked through how AOP saves time via code reuse. For the user to understand AOP, we simplified AOP implementation. In the next chapter, we will talk about how to build a REST client and discuss more about error handling in Spring.

10
Building a REST Client and Error Handling

In previous chapters, we covered the server side of RESTful web services including CRUD operations. Here, we can check how to consume those APIs in the code itself. The REST client will help us to achieve this goal.

In this chapter, we will discuss the following topics:

- RestTemplate in Spring
- Basic setup for building a RESTful service client with Spring
- Calling a RESTful service in the client
- Defining the error handler
- Using the error handler

Building a REST client

So far, we have created a REST API and consumed it in third-party tools such as SoapUI, Postman, or JUnit testing. There might be situations where you will have to consume a REST API using the regular method (service or another controller method) itself like payment API call in service API. It will be useful when you call a third-party API such as PayPal or a weather API in your code. In such situations, having a REST client will be helpful for getting the job done.

Here, we will talk about how to build a REST client to consume another REST API in our method. Before moving onto that, we will talk a little bit about `RestTemplate` in Spring.

RestTemplate

RestTemplate is a Spring class that is used to consume the REST API from the client side through HTTP. By using RestTemplate, we can keep the REST API consumer in the same application as well, so we don't need a third-party application or another application to consume our API. RestTemplate can be used use to call GET, POST, PUT, DELETE, and other advanced HTTP methods (OPTIONS, HEAD).

> By default, the RestTemplate class relies on JDK to establish HTTP connections. You can switch to using a different HTTP library such as Apache HttpComponents and Netty.

First, we will add a RestTemplate bean configuration in the AppConfig class. In the following code, we will see how the RestTemplate bean can be configured:

```
import org.springframework.context.annotation.Bean;
import org.springframework.context.annotation.Configuration;
import org.springframework.web.client.RestTemplate;
@Configuration
public class AppConfig {
  @Bean
  public RestTemplate restTemplate() {
      return new RestTemplate();
  }
}
```

In the preceding code, we have mentioned this class with @Configuration annotation to configure all the beans inside the class. We have also introduced the RestTemplate bean in this class. By configuring the bean in the AppConfig class, we tell the application that the mentioned bean can be used in any place in the application. When the application starts, it is automatically initializing the bean and is ready to use the template wherever needed.

Now, we can use RestTemplate by simply using the @Autowire annotation in any class. For a better understanding, we have created a new class called ClientController and added a simple method in the class:

```
@RestController
@RequestMapping("/client")
public class ClientController {
    private final Logger _log = LoggerFactory.getLogger(this.getClass());
    @Autowired
    RestTemplate template;
    @ResponseBody
```

```
    @RequestMapping("/test")
    public Map<String, Object> test(){
       Map<String, Object> map = new LinkedHashMap<>();
       String content = template.getForObject("http://localhost:8080/",
String.class);
       map.put("result", content);
       return map;
    }
}
```

In the preceding code, we used `RestTemplate` and called the `getForObject` method to consume the API. By default, we used `String.class` to keep our code simple to understand.

When you call this API `http://localhost:8080/client/test/`, you will get the following result:

```
{
    result: "{\"result\":\"Aloha\"}"
}
```

In the preceding process, we have used `RestTemplate` inside another REST API. In a real-time scenario, you might use the same method that you used to call the third-party REST API.

Let's get a single user API inside another method:

```
@ResponseBody
    @RequestMapping("/test/user")
    public Map<String, Object> testGetUser(){
       Map<String, Object> map = new LinkedHashMap<>();
       User user = template.getForObject("http://localhost:8080/user/100",
User.class);
       map.put("result", user);
       return map;
    }
```

By calling the preceding API, you will get the single user as a result. In order to call this API, our `User` class should be serialized, otherwise you might get an unserialized object error. Let's make our `User` class serialized by implementing `Serializable` and adding a serial version ID.

You can create a serial version ID in Eclipse by right-clicking on the class name and generating a serial number.

After serializing the `User` class, it will look as follows:

```java
public class User implements Serializable {
  private static final long serialVersionUID = 3453281303625368221L;
  public User(){
  }
  private Integer userid;
  private String username;
  public User(Integer userid, String username){
    this.userid = userid;
    this.username = username;
  }
  public Integer getUserid() {
    return userid;
  }
  public void setUserid(Integer userid) {
    this.userid = userid;
  }
  public String getUsername() {
    return username;
  }
  public void setUsername(String username) {
    this.username = username;
  }
  @Override
  public String toString() {
    return "User [userid=" + userid + ", username=" + username + "]";
  }
}
```

Finally, we can call the `http://localhost:8080/client/test/user` client API in the browser and get the following result:

```
{
  result: {
    userid: 100,
    username: "David"
  }
}
```

We have used only the `GET` method for ease of understanding. However, we can use the `POST` method and `add` parameters in the REST consumer.

Error handling

So far in our application, we haven't defined any specific error handler to catch the error and convey it to the right format. Usually when we deal with an unexpected situation in REST APIs, it will automatically throw an HTTP error such as 404. Errors such as 404 will show explicitly in the browser. This is fine normally; however, we might need a JSON format result regardless of whether things go right or wrong.

Converting the error into JSON format would be a nice idea in such cases. By providing the JSON format, we can keep our application clean and standardized.

Here, we will discuss how to manage errors and display them in JSON format when things go wrong. Let's create a common error handler class to manage all of our errors:

```
public class ErrorHandler {
  @ExceptionHandler(Exception.class)
  public @ResponseBody <T> T handleException(Exception ex) {
    Map<String, Object> errorMap = new LinkedHashMap<>();
    if(ex instanceof
org.springframework.web.bind.MissingServletRequestParameterException){
      errorMap.put("Parameter Missing", ex.getMessage());
      return (T) errorMap;
    }
    errorMap.put("Generic Error ", ex.getMessage());
    return (T) errorMap;
  }
}
```

The preceding class will act as a common error handler in our application. In the `ErrorHandler` class, we have created a single method called `handleException` with the `@ExceptionHandler` annotation. This annotation will make the method receive all exceptions in the application. Once we get exceptions, we can manage what to do based on the type of exception.

In our code, we have used only two situations to manage our exceptions:

- Missing parameter
- General error (everything else other than missing parameter)

If we miss a parameter when calling any REST API, it will go to the first situation, `Parameter Missing`, or else it will go to the `Generic Error` default error. We have simplified the process to make it understandable for new users. However, we can add more cases in this method to manage more exceptions.

Once we have finished the error handler, we will have to use it in our application. Applying the error handler can be done in many ways. Extending the error handler is the simplest way to use it:

```java
@RestController
@RequestMapping("/")
public class HomeController extends ErrorHandler {
    // other methods
  @ResponseBody
  @RequestMapping("/test/error")
  public Map<String, Object> testError(@RequestParam(value="item") String item) {
     Map<String, Object> map = new LinkedHashMap<>();
     map.put("item", item);
     return map;
  }
}
```

In the preceding code, we just extended `ErrorHandler` in the `HomeController` class. By doing so, we are binding all error scenarios to `ErrorHandler` to receive and handle properly. Also, we have created a test method called `testError` to check our error handler.

In order to call this API, we need to pass `item` as a parameter; otherwise it will throw an error in the application. As we have already defined the `ErrorController` class and extended the `HomeController` class, missing the parameter will take you to the first scenario mentioned earlier.

Just try the following URL in your browser or any REST client (Postman/SoapUI): `http://localhost:8080/test/error`.

If you try the preceding endpoint, you will get the following result:

```
{
  Parameter Missing: "Required String parameter 'item' is not present"
}
```

As we have defined the JSON format in our error handler, if any REST API throws an exception, we will get the error in JSON format.

Customized exception

So far, we have only explored application-thrown errors. However, we can define our own errors and throw them if needed. The following code will show you how to create a customized error and throw it in our application:

```
@RestController
@RequestMapping("/")
public class HomeController extends ErrorHandler {
    // other methods
  @ResponseBody
  @RequestMapping("/test/error/{id}")
  public Map<String, Object> testRuntimeError(@PathVariable("id") Integer id){
     if(id == 1){
        throw new RuntimeException("some exception");
     }
     Map<String, Object> map = new LinkedHashMap<>();
     map.put("result", "one");
     return map;
  }
}
```

In the preceding code, we created a custom exception by using `RuntimeException`. This is just test code to show you how a customized exception works in error handling. We will apply this customized exception in our application in upcoming chapters.

If you call the `http://localhost:8080/test/error/1` API, you will get an error like the one that follows, which is caused by our condition match:

```
{
  Generic Error : "some exception"
}
```

Summary

In this chapter, we learned to build a RESTful web service client using `RestTemplate`. Also, we covered error handlers and centralized error handlers to handle all error-prone scenarios. In upcoming chapters, we will discuss scaling our Spring application and talk a little bit about microservices as those topics are growing rapidly.

11
Scaling

As the world focusses more on the web than ever, all of our web applications will need to service more requests. In order to face the higher number of requests, we might need to scale our applications to support them.

This chapter mainly concentrates on techniques, libraries, and tools that can be applied to our regular applications to address scalability concerns.

In this chapter, we will discuss the following topics:

- Clustering and its benefits
- Load balancing
- Scaling databases
- Distributed caching

Clustering

Simply put, clustering is nothing but adding more than one server to provide the same service. It will help us to avoid interruptions during disasters such as system crashes and other unfortunate situations. Clustering can be used as a failover system, a load balancing system, or a parallel processing unit.

A failover cluster is a group of servers with the sample applications duplicated in all servers to provide the same services to clients to maintain the high availability of applications and services. If a server fails for some reason, the rest of the servers will take over the load and provide uninterrupted services to consumers.

- **Scaling up (vertical scaling)**: This is about adding more resources to our servers, for example, increasing the RAM, hard drive capacity, and processors. Though it might be a good option, it will only be applicable for certain scenarios, not all. In some cases, adding more resources might be expensive.
- **Scaling out (horizontal scaling)**: Unlike adding more resources inside one server, scaling out focuses on adding more servers/nodes to service requests. This grouping is called clustering, as all of the servers are doing the same types of task, but duplicated on different servers to avoid interruption.

Benefits of clustering

Clustering is the more preferred solution for scaling services, as it gives a quick and flexible option to add more servers whenever needed, without interrupting existing services. Uninterrupted service can be provided during scaling. Consumers will not need to wait for anything approaching downtime when scaling the application. All server loads are balanced properly by a central load balancing server.

Load balancing

A load balancer is the most useful tool in clustering. A load balancer uses a variety of algorithms, such as round-robin, least connection, and so on, to forward the incoming request to the right backend servers for processing.

There are a lot of third-party load balancers available on the market, such as F5 (https://f5.com), HAProxy (http://www.haproxy.org), and so on. Though these load balancing tools behave differently, they focus on the main role: distributing the request load to the available backend server and maintaining the balance between all the servers. By proper load balancing, we prevent a single backend server from being overloaded. Also, most load balancers come with health monitoring, such as checks to verify the availability of servicing servers.

Besides the main request distribution among servers, load balancers keep the backend servers protected from frontend servers. Frontend servers will have no idea about which backend server to sent the request to as load balancers hide all details about backend servers.

Scaling databases

Scaling the database is one of the challenging parts of architectural design. Here, we will discuss some database scaling techniques to scale our application.

Vertical scaling

As we discussed earlier, in the application server level we can also utilize the scaling up technique for our database servers. Adding more power, such as CPU and RAM, will bring better performance in querying databases. By using vertical scaling techniques, we can get consistent performance, and it's also easy to debug when things go wrong. Also, vertical scaling offers increased efficiency compared to horizontal scaling. However, vertical scaling might require downtime regularly to install new hardware, and it is limited by the hardware capacity.

Horizontal scaling

As we discussed with horizontal scaling in the application level, we can do the same for database servers by adding more machines to our cluster to take care of the database load. Compared to vertical scaling, it is significantly cheaper; however, this also comes with its own cost structure for cluster configuration, maintenance, and management costs.

Read replicas

By keeping multiple slaves that can be accessed for reading purposes, we can bring significant improvements to our application. Read replicas help to read data in all our slaves that are read-only. However, when we need to send write requests, we can use the master database. A master database can be used for both writing and reading purposes, and slaves can be used only for reading purposes. The more slaves we install, the more read-based queries can be handled. This read replica technique is very useful in scenarios where we have minimal write queries and maximal read queries to be handled.

Pool connections

When an application queries the database, it creates a client connection, sends the query, and gets the results. As the client connection to the database is an expensive operation, the connections must be reused for further queries. Connection pooling will help in this situation by preventing the need establish the connection to the database for each request. By keeping better connection pools, such as HikariCP, we can improve the performance in our applications.

Use multiple masters

Like read replicas, multiple master mechanisms give the option to duplicate multiple database servers. Unlike with read replicas duplicating slaves, here we duplicate master databases to write and read data. This pattern is very useful for specific scenarios such as REST API data transaction-focused applications. In the multiple masters pattern, we require our applications to generate **universally unique identifier** (UUIDs), to prevent data collisions during the multi-master replication process.

Load balancing in DB servers

As the client connection limit from the application server is based on the database vendor, it might be tricky to handle situations when the application servers request more connections. By keeping a load balancer, we can distribute the database queries to available database servers using their connection pools. With the help of a load balancer, we will make sure all database servers are equally loaded; however, it depends on the algorithm used in the specific load balancer.

Database partitioning

Partitioning the database is very helpful when we deal with large databases that require high-end servers and take a lot of time to query. Also, this is useful when our application needs to query large amounts of both read and write requests. Partitioning can be done both horizontally and vertically. Both horizontal and vertical partitioning are described in the following sections.

Sharding (horizontal partitioning)

A database table can be split into multiple tables based on any specific attribute. For example, a user database can be split into two different databases, such as user_1 and user_2, where the user_1 table's username starts with A-N, and the user_2 table's username starts with O-Z. By splitting databases like earlier, we can reduce the number of rows on each table, and hence we can improve the performance.

Vertical partitioning

In vertical partitioning, the database table can be split into many tables, based on business concepts. For example, One table might have more columns to keep other tables to be accessed easily for better performance.

By doing both horizontal and vertical partitioning, querying the database will take less time and improve performance. Also, by dividing a big database into small chunks, we can avoid requiring high-end computers. These data shards can be distributed into low-commodity servers to save money, as well. However, data sharing might be a complex process in specific scenarios.

Distributed caching

Distributed caching techniques will be helpful to improve the scalability in our web services. Unlike in-process caches, distributed caches need not be built in the same application space. They can be stored on multiple nodes of a cluster. Although distributed caches are deployed on multiple nodes, they offer a single state of the cache.

Data-tier caching

Adding a caching layer in the database will provide better performance. It is considered a common strategy for improving performance, especially when read requests are heavy in our application. Here, we will discuss Hibernate's levels of caching.

First-level caching

A first-level cache is an inbuilt session cache enabled by Hibernate, and it is a mandatory cache through all requests. There is no option to disable first-level caching in Hibernate. First-level caching is associated with a session object and will be lost once the session is expired. When we query the web service for the first time, the object is retrieved from the database and stored in the first-level cache, which is associated with the Hibernate session. If we request the same entity again, it will be retrieved from the cache without querying the database.

Second-level caching

The second-level cache is an optional cache in Hibernate. The first-level cache will be the point of contact before our request reaches the second-level cache. The second-level cache can be configured per-class or per-collection, and it is responsible for caching objects across sessions.

As only a few classes benefit from caching, by default second-level caching is disabled. It can be enabled to service designers.

Application-tier caching

Like caching in a database, we can also cache any object in the application layer to improve the performance of the application. Here, we will talk about various object caches, especially key-value caching tools, and check their uniqueness in the market.

Memcached

As most companies use Memcached (https://memcached.org) in their applications, we consider Memcached to be one of the most powerful distributed caching systems. It follows the distributed memory caching mechanism and is very helpful in repeated scenarios, for example, when the same service is requested multiple times.

Redis

Redis (`https://redis.io`) is another in-memory key-value store that can be used for caching. Redis supports data structures such as hashes, lists, sets, and so on. Redis is considered one of the most popular key-value stores, with the support of advanced key-value caches. Redis supports operations such as intersection and union. Because of its advanced capabilities and speed, it is more to be preferred than Memcached.

Hazelcast

Hazelcast (`https://hazelcast.com`) is an in-memory data grid that supports distributed collections and simplifies distributed computing. It provides a simple API with an easy and straightforward deployment strategy. As Hazelcast provides the Memcached client library, applications using a Memcached cluster might be able to adapt to a Hazelcast cluster. Hazelcast architecture supports data distribution and high scalability in a clustered platform. It also provides intelligent synchronization and auto-discovery. Hazelcast offers features such as distributed data structures, distributed queries, and distributed compute. Spring Boot has explicit caching support for Hazelcast in its framework.

Ehcache

Ehcache (`http://www.ehcache.org`)is used mostly in small to medium-scale deployments due to its simplified scalable options. It is considered one of the most widely-used distributed caches. Also, Ehcache provides options to integrate with other popular libraries and frameworks. Ehcache scaling starts from in-process caching and goes through mixed in-process and out-of-process deployments. Also, Ehcache came up with the Terracotta server to improve performance on caching.

Riak

Riak (`https://github.com/basho/riak`) is an Erlang-based key-value data store that is fault-tolerant and gives high availability. In Riak, data can be stored in memory, the disk, or both. Riak can be accessed through protocols such as the HTTP API or Native Erlang interface. Riak supports major languages such as Java, C, and Python. Also, it supports MapReduce, which can be flexible in big data-related operations.

Aerospike

Aerospike (https://www.aerospike.com) is an open source, flash-optimized, in-memory NoSQL database and key-value store. Aerospike operates on three layers: flash-optimized data layer, a self-managed distribution layer, and a cluster-aware client layer. To ensure consistency, the distribution layer is duplicated across all data centers. These duplicates will remain functional even when an individual server node fails or is removed from the cluster.

Infinispan

Infinispan (http://infinispan.org/) is a distributed in-memory key-value data store that can be used as a cache or just a data grid. It can be accessed as a library or over protocols such as REST. Also, Infinispan can be integrated with JPA, JCache, Spring, and Spark. Infinispan supports most MapReduce-related operations.

Cache2k

Cache2k (https://cache2k.org/) provides in-memory object cache options in Java applications. Cache2k mainly focuses on caching inside JVM.

Other distributed caching

Previously, we talked about primary caching tools and their mechanisms. Here, we will discuss more about additional distributed caching that is available on the market:

Amazon ElastiCache

ElastiCache is primarily used as an in-memory data store and cache service; it was introduced by AWS. With the support of Amazon ElastiCache, we can deploy our cache environment quickly, without any complicated installations. It supports both Memcached and Redis caching.

Oracle distributed cache (Coherence)

In this distributed cache, data is partitioned in all computers in the cluster. These partitioned caches will be configured to keep each piece of data on nodes in the cluster. Distributed caches are the most commonly used caches in Coherence.

Even though we have plenty of caching solutions available on the market, selecting a specific solution depends on many factors, such as business requirements, performance requirements, data integrity, fault tolerance, cost, and so on. Adding the right distributed caching layer to the application tier and database tier will result in better performance.

Summary

In this chapter, we talked about different libraries, tools, and techniques to scale a RESTful web service. When developing an application, we will have to look for loose coupling between components of a system by using well-defined interfaces. In the coming chapter, we will talk about microservices and their benefits.

12
Microservice Basics

Though monolithic architecture has its own benefits, when an application is getting bigger to support various types of business logic, it gives a tough time to the developers and deployment engineers. Even a single bug fix in the backend will force the developer to redeploy the whole application in the server, causing unnecessary maintenance. On the other hand, microservices come with an option to keep business logic separated into services. So applications can be pushed to the server without interrupting the flow, and the end user especially should not notice any interruption. In this chapter, we will delve into some basics about microservices and related topics.

In this chapter, we will discuss:

- Monolithic architecture and its drawbacks
- Microservices and their benefits
- Basic characteristics of microservices
- Microservice components
- Microservice tools

Monolithic architecture and its drawbacks

Even though microservice architecture is growing in popularity nowadays, the majority of companies still use the monolithic architecture. As a monolithic application, you can bundle all business modules into one single unit and deploy them in all desired servers. If any changes are needed in the application, developers have to provide them and redeploy the updated version of the application. In monolithic, we follow tight coupling between service modules.

Though monolithic architecture has some benefits, its drawbacks paved the way for an alternate architectural design—microservices. Here we will talk a little about the drawbacks of monolithic architecture:

- For each bug fix or code change, we have to redeploy the entire application on all servers
- If any common issue persists in the monolithic application, such as performance issues, it will impact the entire application, which might be hard to find out and fix quickly
- Bigger applications might take longer to start during deployment
- Library requirements and conflicts might affect the entire application. We will have a hard time fixing libraries to support all modules
- Scaling might be hard for monoliths, as all modules come under one umbrella
- When the application grows, the complexity of business logic and implementation will grow as well, which might need more time to develop and maintain
- Infrequent, expensive, and mass deployment option: if we have multiple types of business logic and layers and want to upgrade one business logic, we will need to deploy all other layers/services, as well
- Tightly coupled services cause difficulty when one service/layer needs an upgrade

Introduction to microservices

Changing a few things in a big application is a constant pain for developers. Every time we make a small change in the code, we might have to deploy the whole application into servers, which is a time-consuming and tiring process, especially when we have multiple services, like accounting, reporting, user management, and so on. Microservices help us get rid of this pain. The main goal of microservices is to split up the application into services and deploy each service to our servers independently. By doing this, we provide loosely coupled processes in our application. Also, microservices can be deployed in the cloud to avoid service outage issues and provide nonstop services to consumers.

In microservices, each module or business section can be written as a separate service to provide continuous delivery and integration. These services are built to fulfill specific business requirements, and they are independently deployable by automating deployment infrastructure. Managing these services can be decentralized and can be programmable in different languages, as well.

Before moving on to components, we will briefly discuss the basic characteristics of microservices.

Independence and autonomy

Microservices play as a better alternative for monolithic environments. In microservices, each service can be started, stopped, upgraded, or replaced at any time, without interrupting other services. All services are independent and can be registered automatically into our central registry.

Resilience and fault tolerance

In a complex application design, creating a resilient system is vital for every service. Most cloud environments require an architectural design where all services respond to unexpected situations, like outages, and so on. These scenarios can be receiving bad data (broken data), may not be able to reach the required service, or may request conflicts in concurrent systems. Microservices need to be resilient to failures, and they should be able to restart themselves quickly.

Microservices should prevent failures from cascading through other dependent services in the system.

Automated environment

Automation should be an important factor in microservice architectural design, as many services will be involved in the application, and thus the interaction between services will be very complex. Automated monitoring and an alert management system have to be implemented to augment microservice design. All services should log their data and metrics, and these metrics should be monitored properly, as it will improve service management.

Stateless

Microservices are stateless, which means they don't keep data from one session to another session. Also, microservice instances will not interact with each other. When we have more microservice instances available in the application, each instance will not have any idea about other instances, whether the next instance is alive or not. This characteristic is very helpful when we scale our applications.

Benefits of microservices

In this section, we will discuss the benefits of developing microservices in our applications:

- Business logic can be grouped and developed into services that are easy to develop and deploy, with multiple service instances
- Microservices can avoid having a complex application by splitting the application into multiple services, providing easy to develop and maintain business logic, especially when we upgrade specific sections
- Services can be deployed independently, without interrupting the application; hence, the end user will never feel any service interruption
- Loosely coupled services will give more flexibility in terms of scaling the application
- Upgrading services separately to meet trendy business requirements is handy, and developers can bring in new technologies to develop the service
- Continuous deployment is easier to implement with the help of microservices; hence, a quick upgrade can be made on desired modules
- Scaling these services will be very flexible, especially when specific business requirements need more instances to provide uninterrupted service to end users in the case of high traffic
- Organizations can focus on small batches of work that they can move to production very quickly, especially when testing out new features for specific clients

Microservice components

In order to have fully functional microservice applications, the following components have to be used properly. These components help us to solve complex business logic distribution among services:

- Configuration server
- Load balancer
- Service discovery
- Circuit breaker
- Edge server

We will briefly discuss these components in this section.

Configuration server

A configuration server will help us store all configurable parameters for each service that will be deployed. These properties can be saved in a repository if needed. Also, the configuration server will give the option to change the configuration of our application without having to deploy the code. Once the configuration is changed, it will be automatically reflected on the fly, so we can avoid redeploying our services.

As we will have many services in our microservice application, having a configuration server will help us to avoid service redeployment, and the service can get the corresponding configuration from the server. It is also one of the principles of continuous delivery: decoupling source code from the configuration.

Load balancer

A load balancer acts as the backbone for scaling applications by allocating the load to specific services. The load balancer is considered a major player in microservice architecture. Unlike regular load balancers distributed among servers, these manage service instances and distribute the load among those instances. With the help of a service discovery component, they will get information about available service instances and distribute the loads.

Netflix Ribbon is used as a load balancer; we will explore this in the *Microservice tools* section of this chapter.

Service discovery

In a microservice architecture, based on the business requirements and service load, we might have to increase the service instances. In such cases, keeping track of all available service instances and their information, such as port numbers, would be hard to manage. Service discovery will help us manage such tasks by automatically configuring service instances and looking them up when in need.

Circuit breaker

As there are many services working together in our architecture, each service might be inter-dependent. There are some situations that cause some services to fail and might be causing other services to fall down with them. To avoid such situations, our architecture should be fault-tolerant. Using patterns like circuit breaker can reduce failures in microservice architectures.

Edge server

The edge server implements the API Gateway pattern, and behaves like a wall for the APIs to the outside world. With the help of an edge server, all public traffic will be forwarded to our internal services. By doing this, end users will not be affected in the case of any changes in our services and internal structures in the future. Netflix Zuul is used as an edge server, and we will share a little bit about Zuul in the following section.

Microservice tools

Netflix engineers contributed much to microservice development and introduced various components for microservice ecosystems. Here, we will discuss more components that might be involved with microservices:

- Netflix Eureka
- Netflix Zuul
- Spring Cloud Config Server
- Netflix Ribbon
- Spring Cloud Netflix
- Spring Security OAuth2

- Netflix Hystrix and Turbine
- Eclipse Microprofile

We will talk more about them in the coming sections.

Netflix Eureka

Eureka plays the role of service discovery service in microservices. It allows microservices to register themselves at runtime and helps us locate services when needed. It is used for the load balancing and fail-over of middle-tier servers. Also, Eureka comes with a Java client (Eureka Client) to make service interaction easier. The Eureka server acts as a middle-tier (services level) load balancing tool by locating services in middle-tier servers. These middle-tier (services level) load balancing tool might not have been available for AWS-like clouds.

Though AWS **Elastic Load Balancer** (**ELB**) is available for load balancing services, it supports only end user web services such as traditional load balancers, not middle-tier load balancing.

In the Eureka server, the instances of the client know which services they have to talk to, as the Eureka load balancer focuses on instance levels as well. Eureka services are stateless, and hence they support scalability. As the server information is cached on the client side, load balancing is very helpful in the case of outages of load balancers.

Eureka is used in Netflix for memcached services, cassandra deployments, and other operations. The Eureka server is highly recommended for middle-tier services where local services should be disabled for the public.

Netflix developers initiated the Eureka server and made it open source. Later, Spring incorporated it into the Spring Cloud. In a microservice architecture, services should be fine-grained to improve the modularity of the application for development, testing, and maintenance.

Netflix Zuul

Zuul acts as a front door gatekeeper to the public, and does not allow unauthorized external requests to pass through. It also provides the entry point to microservices in our server. Zuul uses Netflix Ribbon to lookup available services and routes external requests to the right service instances. Zuul supports dynamic routing, monitoring, and security.

Zuul's different types of filter, like `PRE`, `ROUTING`, `POST`, and `ERROR`, help to achieve the following actions:

- Dynamic routing
- Insights and monitoring
- Authentication and security
- Stress testing
- Multiregion resiliency
- Static response handling

Zuul has multiple components:

- `zuul-core`
- `zuul-simple-webapp`
- `zuul-netflix`
- `zuul-netflix-webapp`

Spring Cloud Netflix

Spring Cloud provides interaction between third-party cloud technologies and the Spring programming model. Spring Cloud Netflix provides Netflix **Open Source Software** (**OSS**) integration support to work with Spring Boot through auto-configuration and binding to the Spring environment. By adding a few annotations in Spring Boot, we can build a large, distributed application, including Netflix components, as well.

Features such as service discovery, service creation, external configuration, router, and filter can be implemented in Spring Cloud Netfix with microservices.

Netflix Ribbon

Netflix is used by service consumers to find services at runtime. Ribbon gets the information from the Eureka server to locate the appropriate service instances. In the case of multiple instances available for Ribbon, it will apply load balancing mechanisms to spread requests over the available instances. Ribbon does not run as a separate service, but rather as an embedded component in each service consumer. Having client-side load balancing is a big benefit from using the service registry as the balancer lets the client pick the registered instance of a service.

Ribbon provides the following features:

- Load balancing rules (multiple and pluggable)
- Service discovery integration
- Resilient over failures
- Support for cloud

Ribbon has sub-components, such as `ribbon-core`, `ribbon-eureka`, and `ribbon-httpclient`.

> Netflix Ribbon acts as a client-side load balancer, and it can be integrated with Spring Cloud.

Netflix Hystrix

Every distributed environment is prone to service failures, which might happen often. In order to fix this issue, our architecture should be fault- and latency-tolerant. Hystrix is a circuit breaker that can help us avoid such situations, like service dependency failures. Hystrix prevents a service from being overloaded and isolates failures when they happen.

With Hystrix support, we can control the interactions between our microservices by adding latency tolerance and fault tolerance logic in them. Hystrix provides strong fallback options in the case of service failure and thus improves our system's overall resiliency. Without Hystrix, if an internal service fails, it might interrupt the API and break the user experience.

Hystrix follows a few basic principles of resiliency, as follows:

- Failure in service dependency should not cause any interruption for the end user
- The API should react in the case of service dependency failure to take correct action

Hystrix also has a circuit breaker fallback mechanism using these approaches:

- **Custom fallback**: Where the client library provides fallback, or local data instead to generate responses
- **Fail silent**: Fallback returns null, which is helpful in some cases
- **Fail fast**: Used in specific cases, such as HTTP 5XX responses

Netflix Turbine

Turbine is used for aggregating all streams of **server-sent-event** (**SSE**) JSON data into one stream, which can be used for dashboard purposes. The Turbine tool is used in the Hystrix application, which has a real-time dashboard to aggregate data from multiple machines. Turbine can be used with any data source that supports the JSON format. Turbine is data-agnostic and able to view the JSON blob as a map of key and value pairs.

Netflix uses Turbine with a Eureka server plugin to handle instances that are joining and leaving clusters for various reasons, like autoscaling, being unhealthy, and so on.

HashiCorp Consul

Consul is a service discovery and configuration tool to support microservices. Consul was initiated by Hashi Corp in 2014, mainly focusing on distributed services across multiple data centers. Also, Consul keeps data safe and works with big infrastructures. By configuring services with keys and values, and finding the services it needs, Consul solves the core problem of microservices.

Consul has servers and clients that form a single Consul cluster. In the Consul cluster, nodes will be able to store and replicate data. Discovering other members in the cluster happens automatically, with the help of at least one member's address. Also, Consul provides a dynamic infrastructure, so there is no extra coding/development needed for the auto-discovery of services.

Consul is made for both the DevOps community and application developers to support modern and elastic infrastructures.

Eclipse MicroProfile

Eclipse MicroProfile was initiated by companies such as RedHat, IBM, and other groups, to provide a specification for building microservices. This project was started in 2016, and recently they have released the 1.2 version of MicroProfile. It mainly focuses on optimizing enterprise Java for microservice architectures. Both Payara Micro and Payara Servers are compatible with Eclipse MicroProfile.

Eclipse MicroProfile version 1.2 comes with a config API, health checks, fault tolerance, metrics, and other necessary tools to support microservices.

Summary

In this chapter, we have briefly discussed monoliths and their drawbacks. We then talked about microservices and their benefits, and related topics. Also, we talked about the basic principles of microservices, including resilience and fault tolerance.

In the later section of this chapter, we talked about microservice components and covered tools involved with microservices, such as Netflix Eureka, Zuul, and so on. In the next and final chapter, we will work on a Ticket management real-time scenario, with advanced CRUD operations, including authentication and authorization.

13
Ticket Management – Advanced CRUD

Our application has to meet real-time business cases, such as Ticket management. This chapter will review most of the topics covered in the book's previous chapters.

In this chapter, we will create a real-time scenario and implement the business requirements for our scenario—Ticket management by the user, **customer service representative (CSR)**, and admin.

Our final chapter includes the following topics:

- Creating a ticket by customer
- Updating the ticket by customer, CSR, and admin
- Deleting the ticket by customer
- CSR/admin deletes multiple tickets

Ticket management using CRUD operations

Before moving on to the Ticket Management System, we will cover business requirements.

Let's say we have a banking web application that can be used by our customers, Peter and Kevin, and we have Sammy, our admin, and Chloe, the CSR, to help in case of any application issues.

Peter and Kevin are facing some problems in the payment process. When they try to click on the payment transaction submit button, it's not working. Also, the transaction view is in a web page. So our users (Peter and Kevin) will create a ticket to share their problem.

Once the ticket is created, it can be updated by customer/CSR/admin. Also, a customer can delete their own ticket. While updating, anyone can change the severity; however, only CSR and admin can change the status, as the ticket's status is related to official activities.

Customers can view their tickets in total or as a single ticket, but they can delete only one ticket at a time. The Multi-delete option is available for both CSR and admin. However, CSR can only delete three tickets at once. Admin will have full control in the Ticket management application and can delete any number of tickets at any time.

Registration

Let's start our coding to fulfill the preceding requirements. At first, we need to start with customer, CSR, and admin registration. As these users have different roles, we will give different user types for each user.

User types

To differentiate users, we came up with three different user types so their authorization will be varied when they access our REST APIs. Here are the three different user types:

Name	User type
General user/customer	1
CSR	2
Admin	3

User POJO

In our previous `User` class, we only had the `userid` and `username`. We may need two more variables to fulfill the business requirements we mentioned earlier. We will add `password` and `usertype` to our existing `User` class:

```
    private String password;
      /*
       * usertype:
       * 1 - general user
       * 2 - CSR (Customer Service Representative)
       * 3 - admin
       */
```

```
private Integer usertype;
public String getPassword() {
    return password;
}
public void setPassword(String password) {
   this.password = password;
}
public void setUsertype(Integer usertype){
    this.usertype = usertype;
}
public Integer getUsertype(){
    return this.usertype;
}
```

In the preceding code, we have just added `password` and `usertype`. Also, we have added getter and setter methods for our variables.

> You can view the full `User` class on our GitHub repository (https://github.com/PacktPublishing/Building-RESTful-Web-Services-with-Spring-5-Second-Edition).

> You may be tired of adding getter and setter methods, so we will replace them with Lombok library, which we will discuss later in this chapter. However, Lombok library has some conflict issues with Eclipse or STS IDE, which you might need to be aware of. In certain versions of these IDEs, you won't get expected behavior on class creation because of Lombok library issues. Also, some developers mentioned that they have deployment issues with Lombok.

In order to automatically generate user ID from our `User` class, we will use a separate counter. We will keep a static variable to do that; it's not recommended in real application to keep a static counter. To simplify our implementation logic, we have used the static counter.

The following code will be added to our `User` class:

```
private static Integer userCounter = 100;
```

We have started with 100 users. Whenever a new user is added, it will automatically increment the `userid` and assign it to the new user.

There is no restriction on the `userCounter` starting point. By keeping user series in 2 (2XX) and ticket in series 3 (3XX), it's easier for the reader to differentiate user and ticket.

Now we will create a new constructor to add the user to our application. Also, we shall increment the `usercounter` parameter and assign it as `userid` for each new user:

```
public User(String username, String password, Integer usertype) {
    userCounter++;
    this.userid = userCounter;
    this.username = username;
    this.password = password;
    this.usertype = usertype;
}
```

The preceding constructor will fill all user details, including the `userid` (from `usercounter`).

Here, we will add a new user with `username`, `password`, and `usertype` in the `UserServiceImpl` class; `usertype` will vary for each user (for example, `usertype` for admin is 3):

```
@Override
public void createUser(String username, String password, Integer usertype) {
    User user = new User(username, password, usertype);
    this.users.add(user);
}
```

In the preceding code, we have created a new user and added it to the existing user list.

In the preceding code, we didn't mention the abstract method in `UserService`. It is assumed that every concrete method will have an abstract method in the interface. Hereafter, consider adding all abstract methods in appropriate interfaces.

Customer registration

Now it is time to add a customer. A new customer will have to create an account by adding a username and password details.

We will talk about the customer registration API. This API will help any new customer to register their account with us:

```
@ResponseBody
@RequestMapping(value = "/register/customer", method = RequestMethod.POST)
public Map<String, Object> registerCustomer(
    @RequestParam(value = "username") String username,
    @RequestParam(value = "password") String password
) {
    userSevice.createUser(username, password, 1);
    return Util.getSuccessResult();
}
```

In the preceding code, we have added an API to register a customer. Whoever is calling this API will be considered a customer (not admin/CSR). As you can see, we have mentioned 1 as the `usertype`, so it will be considered a customer.

Here's the screenshot of SoapUI for customer registration:

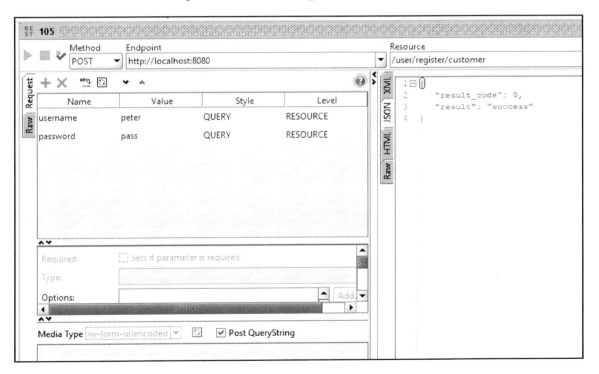

Also, in the preceding code, we have used `getSuccessResult` from our `Util` class. We will see other `Util` methods, shown in the following code:

```
package com.packtpub.util;
import java.util.LinkedHashMap;
import java.util.Map;
public class Util {
  public static <T> T getUserNotAvailableError(){
    Map<String, Object> map = new LinkedHashMap<>();
    map.put("result_code", 501);
    map.put("result", "User Not Available");
    return (T) map;
  }
  public static <T> T getSuccessResult(){
    Map<String, Object> map = new LinkedHashMap<>();
    map.put("result_code", 0);
    map.put("result", "success");
    return (T) map;
  }
  public static <T> T getSuccessResult(Object obj){
    Map<String, Object> map = new LinkedHashMap<>();
    map.put("result_code", 0);
    map.put("result", "success");
    map.put("value", obj);
    return (T) map;
  }
}
```

In the preceding code, we created a `Util` class to keep generic methods that will be used in different controllers, such as `Ticket` and `User`. These `Util` methods are used to avoid code duplication in our application.

> To simplify the flow, we haven't used any exception-handling mechanism in this code. You may need to implement the methods with proper exception handling-techniques.

Admin registration

Every application will have an admin to control all actions, such as deleting the customer and changing status. Here, we will talk about the admin registration API.

The admin registration API will also use the `createUser` method to create admin. Here's the code for admin registration:

```
@ResponseBody
@RequestMapping(value = "/register/admin", method = RequestMethod.POST)
public Map<String, Object> registerAdmin(
    @RequestParam(value = "username") String username,
    @RequestParam(value = "password") String password
) {
    Map<String, Object> map = new LinkedHashMap<>();
    userSevice.createUser(username, password, 3); // 3 - admin (usertype)
    map.put("result", "added");
    return map;
}
```

In the preceding code, we have added code for admin registration while mentioning 3 (user type for admin) in the `createUser` constructor call. Also, you can see that we use the POST method for registration.

The following is the screenshot for the `http://localhost:8080/user/register/admin` admin registration SoapUI API call:

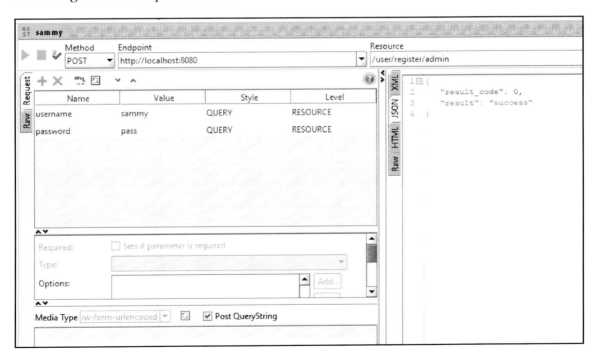

Ticket Management – Advanced CRUD

 In our Ticket management, we didn't have any restrictions on duplicating the user, which means we can have many users with the same name. We recommend that you avoid duplicating them, as this will disrupt the flow. To simplify our implementation as much as possible, we have ignored such restrictions. However, you can implement the restriction to improve the application.

CSR registration

In this section, we will talk about CSR registration.

There is only one difference in customer registration—usertype. Other than usertype and API path, nothing is different from the other registration calls:

```
@ResponseBody
@RequestMapping(value = "/register/csr", method = RequestMethod.POST)
public Map<String, Object> registerCSR(
    @RequestParam(value = "username") String username,
    @RequestParam(value = "password") String password
) {
    userSevice.createUser(username, password, 2);
    return Util.getSuccessResult();
}
```

As we did with the other APIs, we have used 2 (user type for CSR) to register a CSR. Let's see the API call in SoapUI, as follows:

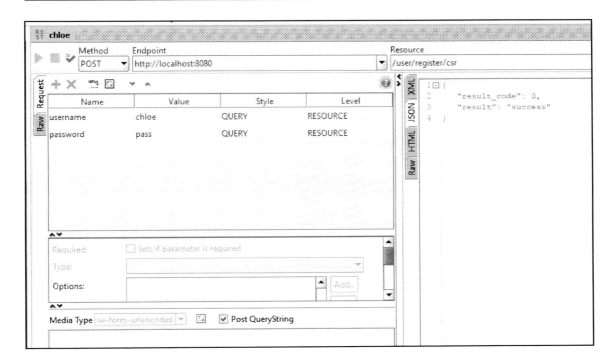

Login and token management

In the last section, we have covered user registration topics, such as customer, admin, and CSR. Once the user is successfully registered, they will have to log in to perform an action. So, let's create login- and session-related API and business implementations.

Before moving to login and session, we will talk about JSON Web Token, which will be used for session authentication. As we already have the createToken method in our securityService class, we will only talk about the subject used in token generation.

Generating a token

We may need to use the JSON Web Token for session purposes. We will use our existing token generation method to keep our user details:

```
        String subject = user.getUserid()+"="+user.getUsertype();
        String token = securityService.createToken(subject, (15 * 1000 * 60));
// 15 mins expiry time
```

We have used `user.getUserid()+"="+user.getUsertype()` as a subject. Also, we have mentioned 15 minutes as an expiry time, so the token will be valid for only 15 minutes.

Customer login

Let's create a login API for customers. The customer has to provide the username and password details as parameters. In a real application, these details might come from an HTML form as follows:

```
@ResponseBody
@RequestMapping(value = "/login/customer", method = RequestMethod.POST)
public Map<String, Object> loginCustomer(
    @RequestParam(value = "username") String username,
    @RequestParam(value = "password") String password
) {
  User user = userSevice.getUser(username, password, 1);
  if(user == null){
    return Util.getUserNotAvailableError();
  }
  String subject = user.getUserid()+"="+user.getUsertype();
  String token = securityService.createToken(subject, (15 * 1000 * 60));
// 15 minutes expiry time
  return Util.getSuccessResult(token);
}
```

In the preceding code, we have called the `getUser` method from `userService` by passing all the necessary parameters. As the user type is 1, we have passed 1 in our method. Once we get the user, we have checked whether it's null or not. If null, we will simply throw the error. If the user is not null, we create a token subject (`user.getUserid()+"="+user.getUsertype()`) and create a token with 15 minutes expiry time, as we mentioned earlier.

If everything goes as we expected, we will create a result map and return the map as an API response. This map will be shown as a JSON response in our result when we call this API.

Also, in the preceding code, we have used `getUserNotAvailableError` to return error details. As we will be using this error in all session-related APIs, we have created a separate method to avoid code duplication.

Here, we can see the customer login SoapUI screenshot:

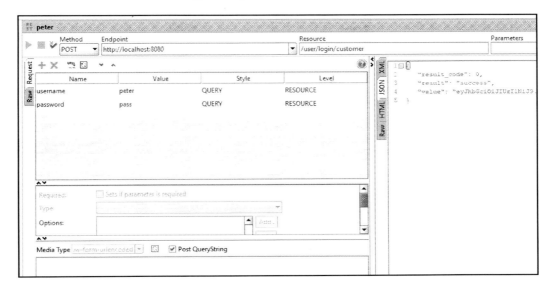

In case of a successful user login, we will get a token in the response JSON. We will have to use the token for session-related APIs, such as add ticket. A sample token is given here:
eyJhbGciOiJIUzI1NiJ9.eyJzdWIiOiIxMDM9MSIsImV4cCI6MTUxNTg5MDMzN30.v9wtiG-fNWlpjgJmou7w2oxA9XjXywsH32cDZ-P4zM4

In some methods, we may see the `<T>` T return type that is a part of Java generics. By keeping such generics, we can return any object by casting it properly.
Here's a sample:
The `return (T) map;` return type

Admin login

As we have seen the customer login section, we will also have a login API for admin.

Here, we will create an API for admin login and generate a token after successful authentication:

```
@ResponseBody
@RequestMapping(value = "/login/admin", method = RequestMethod.POST)
public Map<String, Object> loginAdmin(
```

Ticket Management – Advanced CRUD

```
        @RequestParam(value = "username") String username,
        @RequestParam(value = "password") String password
    ) {
    Map<String, Object> map = new LinkedHashMap<>();
    User user = userSevice.getUser(username, password, 3);
    if(user == null){
      return Util.getUserNotAvailableError();
    }
    String subject = user.getUserid()+"="+user.getUsertype();
    String token = securityService.createToken(subject, (15 * 1000 * 60));
// 15 mins expiry time
    map.put("result_code", 0);
    map.put("result", "success");
    map.put("token", token);
    return map;
  }
```

The preceding login API will be used only for admin purposes. We have used `usertype` as 3 to create an admin user. Also, we have used the `Util` method `getUserNotAvailableError`.

Here's the SoapUI screenshot for the admin login:

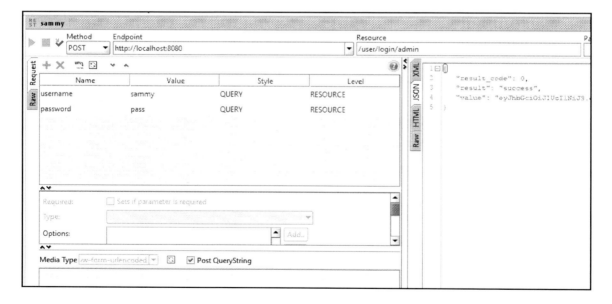

CSR login

In this section, we will talk about CSR login and token generation for CSR in `TicketController`:

```
    @ResponseBody
    @RequestMapping(value = "/login/csr", method = RequestMethod.POST)
    public Map<String, Object> loginCSR(
        @RequestParam(value = "username") String username,
        @RequestParam(value = "password") String password
    ) {
    User user = userSevice.getUser(username, password, 2);
    if(user == null){
        return Util.getUserNotAvailableError();
    }
    String subject = user.getUserid()+"="+user.getUsertype();
    String token = securityService.createToken(subject, (15 * 1000 * 60));
// 15 mins expiry time

    return Util.getSuccessResult(token);
    }
```

As usual, we will get the user from our list and check for null. If the user is not available, we will throw an error, otherwise the code will fall through. As we did with other user types, we will create a separate API for CSR and pass `usertype` as 1 to create a CSR.

You can see the CSR login API in the following screenshot:

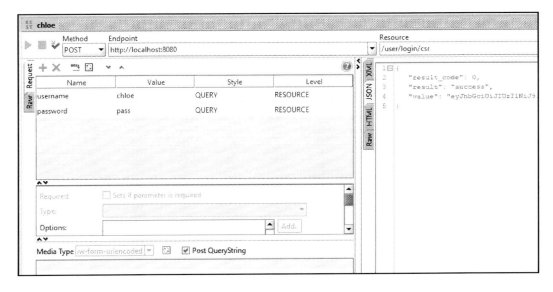

Ticket management

In order to create a ticket, we need to create a `Ticket` class and store the tickets in the list. We will talk more about the `Ticket` class, ticket list, and other ticket-related work, such as user Ticket management, admin Ticket management, and CSR Ticket management.

Ticket POJO

We will create a `Ticket` class with some basic variables involved to store all details related to ticket. The following code will help us understand the `Ticket` class:

```java
public class Ticket {
  private Integer ticketid;
  private Integer creatorid;
  private Date createdat;
  private String content;
  private Integer severity;
  private Integer status;
  // getter and setter methods
  @Override
  public String toString() {
    return "Ticket [ticketid=" + ticketid + ", creatorid=" + creatorid
        + ", createdat=" + createdat + ", content=" + content
        + ", severity=" + severity + ", status=" + status + "]";
  }
  private static Integer ticketCounter = 300;
  public Ticket(Integer creatorid, Date createdat, String content, Integer severity, Integer status){
    ticketCounter++;
    this.ticketid = ticketCounter;
    this.creatorid = creatorid;
    this.createdat = createdat;
    this.content = content;
    this.severity = severity;
    this.status = status;
  }
}
```

The preceding code will store ticket details such as `ticketid`, `creatorid`, `createdat`, `content`, `severity`, and `status`. Also, we have used a static counter called `ticketCounter` to increment the `ticketid` upon ticket creation. By default, it will start with 300.

Also, we have used a constructor and the `toString` method, as we will be using them in our implementation.

We will have to create the `TicketService` interface (for abstract methods) and the `TicketServiceImpl` concrete class for all ticket-related business logic implementation.

The following code will show how to add a ticket:

```
@Override
public void addTicket(Integer creatorid, String content, Integer severity, Integer status) {
   Ticket ticket = new Ticket(creatorid, new Date(), content, severity, status);
   tickets.add(ticket);
}
```

In the preceding code snippet, we just used our constructor to create a ticket and add the ticket to our list. We can clearly see that we haven't used `ticketid` as created by the incrementer in the `Ticket` class. Once the ticket is created, we add it to the ticket list, which will be used for other operations.

Getting a user by token

For all ticket-related operations, we need the user session. In the login method, we got the token after successful logging in. We can use the token to get the user details. If the token is not available, not matched, or expired, we won't be able to get the user details.

Here, we will implement the method to get the user details from the token:

```
@Override
public User getUserByToken(String token){
   Claims claims = Jwts.parser()
.setSigningKey(DatatypeConverter.parseBase64Binary(SecurityServiceImpl.secretKey))
         .parseClaimsJws(token).getBody();
   if(claims == null || claims.getSubject() == null){
     return null;
   }
   String subject = claims.getSubject();
   if(subject.split("=").length != 2){
     return null;
   }
   String[] subjectParts = subject.split("=");
   Integer usertype = new Integer(subjectParts[1]);
   Integer userid = new Integer(subjectParts[0]);
```

```
        return new User(userid, usertype);
    }
```

In the preceding code, we have used the token to get the user details. We are using JWT parser to get the claim first, and then we will get the subject. If you remember, we have used `user.getUserid()+"="+user.getUsertype()` as a subject when we created a token for all user login options. So the subject will be in the same format, for example, 101 (user ID)=1 (user type) for a customer, as the customer's user type is 1.

Also, we do check whether the subject is valid or not with `subject.split("=").length != 2`. In case we use a different token, it will simply return null.

Once we get the proper subject, we will get the `userid` and `usertype`, and then we will return the user by creating a `User` object.

> Because `getUserByToken` is common for all users, it will be used for all of our user retrieval methods.

User Ticket management

First of all, to simplify our business requirements, we keep the rule that only customers can create a ticket. Neither admin nor CSR can create a ticket. In real-time situations, you may have different approaches to Ticket management. However, we will keep the business requirements as simple as possible.

Ticket controller

Here, we will discuss creating a ticket by a customer:

```
/*
 * Rule:
 * Only user can create a ticket
 */
@SuppressWarnings("unchecked")
@ResponseBody
@UserTokenRequired
@RequestMapping(value = "", method = RequestMethod.POST)
public <T> T addTicket(
    @RequestParam(value="content") String content,
    HttpServletRequest request
```

```
        ) {
    User user = userSevice.getUserByToken(request.getHeader("token"));
    ticketSevice.addTicket(user.getUserid(), content, 2, 1);
    return Util.getSuccessResult();
}
```

When the user submits a ticket, they will send only the details about what problem they face in the application. We have provided the content variable for such details. Also, we get the user details from the token they pass in the header.

We can see the success response in the following screenshot:

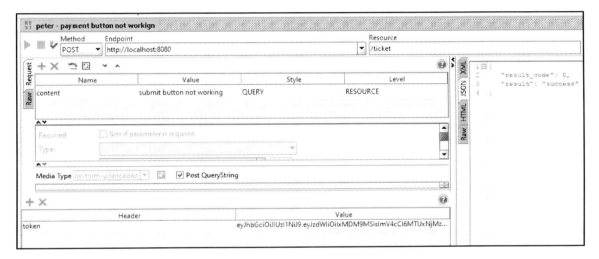

In the previous API, we have used the @UserTokenRequired annotation to validate the user token. We will check the details of annotation and implementation here.

The UserTokenRequired interface

Here, we will introduce the UserTokenRequired interface and follow up with validation logic in the next section:

```
package com.packtpub.aop;
import java.lang.annotation.ElementType;
import java.lang.annotation.Retention;
import java.lang.annotation.RetentionPolicy;
import java.lang.annotation.Target;
@Retention(RetentionPolicy.RUNTIME)
@Target(ElementType.METHOD)
```

```
public @interface UserTokenRequired {
}
```

The UserTokenRequiredAspect class
This class will check the user token for user ID and user type validation after decrypting it:

```
package com.packtpub.aop;
import javax.servlet.http.HttpServletRequest;
import javax.xml.bind.DatatypeConverter;
import org.aspectj.lang.annotation.Aspect;
import org.aspectj.lang.annotation.Before;
import org.springframework.stereotype.Component;
import org.springframework.util.StringUtils;
import org.springframework.web.context.request.RequestContextHolder;
import org.springframework.web.context.request.ServletRequestAttributes;
import com.packtpub.service.SecurityServiceImpl;
import io.jsonwebtoken.Claims;
import io.jsonwebtoken.Jwts;
@Aspect
@Component
public class UserTokenRequiredAspect {
  @Before("@annotation(userTokenRequired)")
  public void tokenRequiredWithAnnotation(UserTokenRequired userTokenRequired) throws Throwable{
    ServletRequestAttributes reqAttributes = (ServletRequestAttributes)RequestContextHolder.currentRequestAttributes();
    HttpServletRequest request = reqAttributes.getRequest();
    // checks for token in request header
    String tokenInHeader = request.getHeader("token");
    if(StringUtils.isEmpty(tokenInHeader)){
      throw new IllegalArgumentException("Empty token");
    }
    Claims claims = Jwts.parser()
.setSigningKey(DatatypeConverter.parseBase64Binary(SecurityServiceImpl.secretKey))
            .parseClaimsJws(tokenInHeader).getBody();
    if(claims == null || claims.getSubject() == null){
      throw new IllegalArgumentException("Token Error : Claim is null");
    }
    String subject = claims.getSubject();
    if(subject.split("=").length != 2){
      throw new IllegalArgumentException("User token is not authorized");
    }
  }
}
```

In the preceding `UserTokenRequiredAspect` class, we have just got the token from the header and verified whether the token is valid or not. If the token is invalid, we will throw an exception.

If the user is null (perhaps there is a wrong or empty token), it will return `"User Not Available"` in the response. Once the necessary token is provided, we will add the ticket by calling the `addTicket` method in `TicketServiceImpl`, which we mentioned earlier.

> Severity levels are as follows:
>
> - Minor: Level 1
> - Normal: Level 2
> - Major: Level 3
> - Critical: Level 4
>
> Level 1 is considered low, and level 4 is considered high, as seen here `@SuppressWarnings ("unchecked")`. In some places, we might have used the `@SuppressWarnings` annotation where we need to tell the compiler that it doesn't need to worry about proper casting, as it will be taken care of.

If the user passes the wrong JWT in any session-related APIs, we will get the error, as follows:

```
{
    "timestamp": 1515786810739,
    "status": 500,
    "error": "Internal Server Error",
    "exception": "java.lang.IllegalArgumentException",
    "message": "JWT String argument cannot be null or empty.",
    "path": "/ticket"
}
```

The preceding error simply mentions that the JWT string is empty or null.

Getting my tickets – customer

Once the ticket is created, the customer can see their tickets by calling the /my/tickets API. The following method will handle the get ticket requirements:

```
@ResponseBody
@RequestMapping("/my/tickets")
public Map<String, Object> getMyTickets(
    HttpServletRequest request
    ) {
  User user = userSevice.getUserByToken(request.getHeader("token"));
  if(user == null){
    return Util.getUserNotAvailableError();
  }
  return
Util.getSuccessResult(ticketSevice.getMyTickets(user.getUserid()));
}
```

In the preceding code, we have validated the user session by token and got the tickets for the user available in the session:

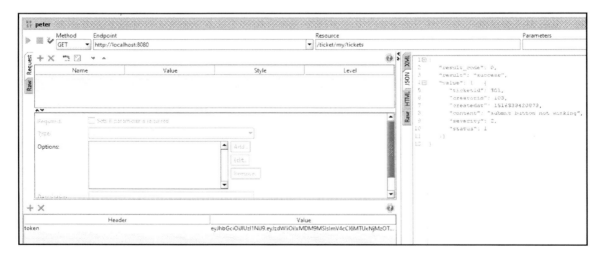

Allowing a user to view their single ticket

Like viewing all customer tickets, customers also can view each of their own ticket details by calling the /{ticketid} API. Let's see how his method works:

```
@ResponseBody
@TokenRequired
@RequestMapping("/{ticketid}")
public <T> T getTicket(
   @PathVariable("ticketid") final Integer ticketid,
   HttpServletRequest request
   ) {
   return (T) Util.getSuccessResult(ticketSevice.getTicket(ticketid));
}
```

In the preceding API, after validating the session, we have used the `getTicket` method in `TicketServiceImpl` to get the user ticket details.

You can verify the result with the help of this screenshot:

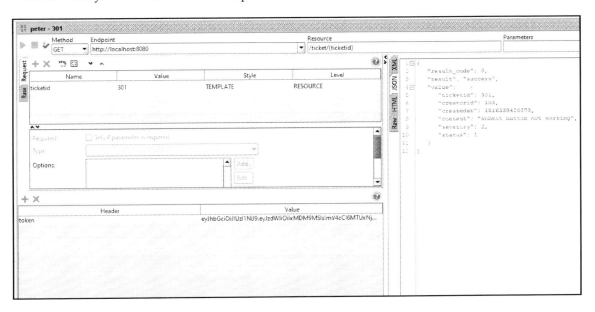

You can clearly see that the token is used in our header. Without the token, the API will throw an exception, as it is a session-related transaction.

Ticket Management – Advanced CRUD

Allowing a customer to update a ticket

Let's assume that the customer wants to update their own ticket for some reason, such as adding extra information. We will be given an option for the customer to update the ticket.

Updating a ticket – service (TicketServiceImpl)

For the updating option, we will add the `updateTicket` method to our `TicketServiceImpl` class:

```
@Override
public void updateTicket(Integer ticketid, String content, Integer severity, Integer status) {
   Ticket ticket = getTicket(ticketid);
   if(ticket == null){
      throw new RuntimeException("Ticket Not Available");
   }
   ticket.setContent(content);
   ticket.setSeverity(severity);
   ticket.setStatus(status);
}
```

In the preceding method, we retrieved the ticket by the `getTicket` method and then updated the necessary information such as `content`, `severity`, and `status`.

Now we can use the `updateTicket` method in our API, which is mentioned here:

```
@ResponseBody
@RequestMapping(value = "/{ticketid}", method = RequestMethod.PUT)
public <T> T updateTicketByCustomer (
    @PathVariable("ticketid") final Integer ticketid,
    @RequestParam(value="content") String content,
    HttpServletRequest request,
    HttpServletResponse response
    ) {
  User user = userSevice.getUserByToken(request.getHeader("token"));
  if(user == null){
     return getUserNotAvailableError();
  }
  ticketSevice.updateTicket(ticketid, content, 2, 1);
  Map<String, String> result = new LinkedHashMap<>();
  result.put("result", "updated");
  return (T) result;
}
```

[188]

In the preceding code, after validating the session, we called `updateTicket` and passed the new content. Also, upon successful completion, we sent the proper response to the caller.

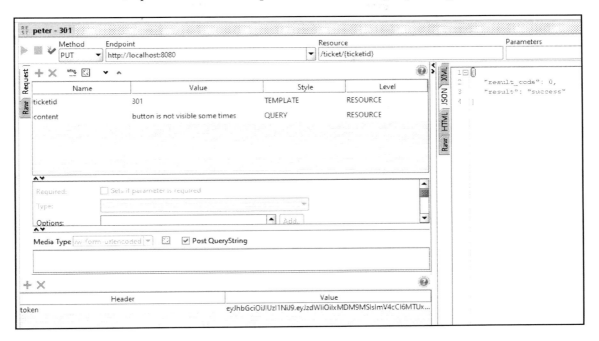

 For the updating option, we have used the `PUT` method, as it is the appropriate HTTP method for updating purposes. However, we can also use the `POST` method for such operations, as there is no restriction on it.

Deleting a ticket

So far, we have covered the create, read, and update actions of a ticket. In this section, we will talk about the delete option for the customer.

Deleting a service – service (TicketServiceImpl)

We will add the `deleteMyTicket` method in our `TicketServiceImpl` class, assuming that we have already added the abstract method to our interface:

```
@Override
  public void deleteMyTicket(Integer userid, Integer ticketid) {
     tickets.removeIf(x -> x.getTicketid().intValue() == ticketid.intValue()
&& x.getCreatorid().intValue() == userid.intValue());
  }
```

In the preceding code, we have used the `removeIf` Java Streams option to find and remove the item from the stream. If the userid and ticket is matched, the item will automatically be removed from the stream.

Deleting my ticket – API (ticket controller)

We can call the `deleteMyTicket` method that we created earlier in our API:

```
@ResponseBody
@UserTokenRequired
@RequestMapping(value = "/{ticketid}", method = RequestMethod.DELETE)
public <T> T deleteTicketByUser (
    @RequestParam("ticketid") final Integer ticketid,
    HttpServletRequest request
    ) {
  User user = userSevice.getUserByToken(request.getHeader("token"));
  ticketSevice.deleteMyTicket(user.getUserid(), ticketid);
  return Util.getSuccessResult();
}
```

As usual, we will check the session and call the `deleteTicketByUser` method in our `TicketServiceImpl` class. Once the delete option is finished, we will simply return the map that says `"success"` as a result.

Here's the SoapUI response after deleting the ticket:

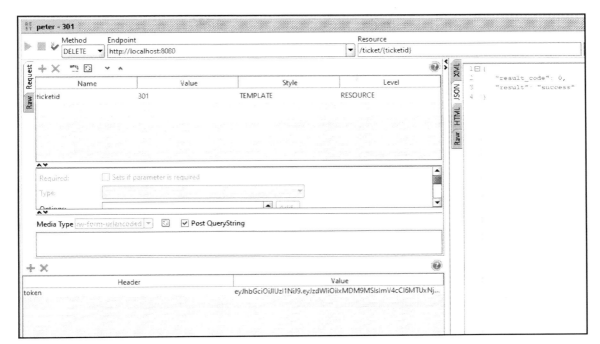

 In our ticket CRUD, we don't have an option to throw an exception when it is empty. If you delete all of your existing tickets and call get tickets, you will get a success message with empty values. You can improve the application by adding an empty check and restrictions.

Admin Ticket management

In the previous section, we saw Ticket management by the customer. The customer has control over their tickets alone and can't do anything with other customers' tickets. In the admin mode, we can have control over any tickets available in the application. In this section, we'll see Ticket management done by admin.

Allowing a admin to view all tickets

As admin has full control to view all tickets in the application, we keep the view ticket method very simple in `TicketServiceImpl` class without any restrictions.

Getting all tickets – service (TicketServiceImpl)

Here we will discuss about the admin implementation part to get all the tickets in the application:

```
@Override
public List<Ticket> getAllTickets() {
  return tickets;
}
```

In the preceding code, we don't have any specific restrictions and simply return all tickets from our ticket list.

Getting all tickets – API (ticket controller)

In the ticket controller API, we will add a method to get all the tickets for admin:

```
@ResponseBody
@AdminTokenRequired
@RequestMapping("/by/admin")
public <T> T getAllTickets(
  HttpServletRequest request,
  HttpServletResponse response) {
  return (T) ticketSevice.getAllTickets();
}
```

The preceding API, `/by/admin` will be called when the admin needs to view all tickets. We have called the `getAllTickets` method in our `TicketServiceImpl` class.

We have used a simple AOP for validating the admin token called `@AdminTokenRequired`. Let's see the implementation part of this API.

The AdminTokenRequired interface

The `AdminTokenRequired` interface will be the base for our implementation, which we will cover later:

```
package com.packtpub.aop;
import java.lang.annotation.ElementType;
import java.lang.annotation.Retention;
import java.lang.annotation.RetentionPolicy;
import java.lang.annotation.Target;
@Retention(RetentionPolicy.RUNTIME)
@Target(ElementType.METHOD)
```

```
public @interface AdminTokenRequired {
}
```

In the preceding code, we introduced the interface for validating an admin token. The validation method will follow up in the `AdminTokenRequiredAspect` class.

The AdminTokenRequiredAspect class

In the aspect class, we will do the validation of an admin token:

```
package com.packtpub.aop;
import javax.servlet.http.HttpServletRequest;
import javax.xml.bind.DatatypeConverter;
import org.aspectj.lang.annotation.Aspect;
import org.aspectj.lang.annotation.Before;
import org.springframework.stereotype.Component;
import org.springframework.util.StringUtils;
import org.springframework.web.context.request.RequestContextHolder;
import org.springframework.web.context.request.ServletRequestAttributes;
import com.packtpub.service.SecurityServiceImpl;
import io.jsonwebtoken.Claims;
import io.jsonwebtoken.Jwts;
@Aspect
@Component
public class AdminTokenRequiredAspect {
  @Before("@annotation(adminTokenRequired)")
  public void adminTokenRequiredWithAnnotation(AdminTokenRequired adminTokenRequired) throws Throwable{
    ServletRequestAttributes reqAttributes = (ServletRequestAttributes)RequestContextHolder.currentRequestAttributes();
    HttpServletRequest request = reqAttributes.getRequest();
    // checks for token in request header
    String tokenInHeader = request.getHeader("token");
    if(StringUtils.isEmpty(tokenInHeader)){
      throw new IllegalArgumentException("Empty token");
    }
    Claims claims = Jwts.parser().setSigningKey(DatatypeConverter.parseBase64Binary(SecurityServiceImpl.secretKey))
            .parseClaimsJws(tokenInHeader).getBody();
    if(claims == null || claims.getSubject() == null){
      throw new IllegalArgumentException("Token Error : Claim is null");
    }
    String subject = claims.getSubject();
    if(subject.split("=").length != 2 || new Integer(subject.split("=")[1]) != 3){
```

Ticket Management – Advanced CRUD

```
            throw new IllegalArgumentException("User is not authorized");
        }
    }
}
```

In the preceding code, we have provided the token validation technique in the `AdminTokenRequiredAspect` class. This aspect component will be executed before the method execution. Also, in this method, we checked the token for empty and null as well as the user type of the token.

Check the SoapUI response for tickets view by admin:

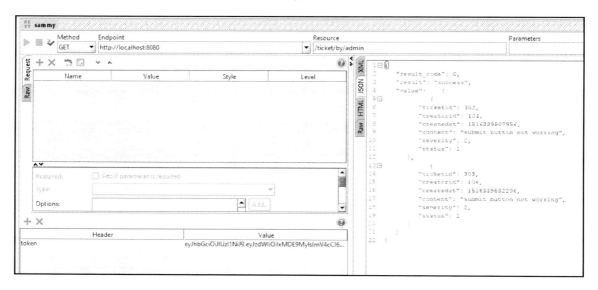

If we use the wrong token or an empty token, we will get a response like this:

```
{
    "timestamp": 1515803861286,
    "status": 500,
    "error": "Internal Server Error",
    "exception": "java.lang.RuntimeException",
    "message": "User is not authorized",
    "path": "/ticket/by/admin"
}
```

By keeping an AOP annotation, we can have a few lines on each method, as the annotation will take care of the business logic.

Admin updates a ticket

Once the ticket is created, it can be viewed by the admin. Unlike a customer, admin has more control to update the ticket status and severity in addition to its content.

Updating a ticket by admin – service (TicketServiceImpl)

Here we will implement the method for ticket update by admin:

```
@ResponseBody
@RequestMapping(value = "/by/admin", method = RequestMethod.PUT)
public <T> T updateTicketByAdmin (
    @RequestParam("ticketid") final Integer ticketid,
    @RequestParam(value="content") String content,
    @RequestParam(value="severity") Integer severity,
    @RequestParam(value="status") Integer status,
    HttpServletRequest request,
    HttpServletResponse response
    ) {
  User user = userSevice.getUserByToken(request.getHeader("token"));
  if(user == null){
    return getUserNotAvailableError();
  }
  ticketSevice.updateTicket(ticketid, content, severity, status);
  Map<String, String> result = new LinkedHashMap<>();
  result.put("result", "updated");
  return (T) result;
}
```

In the preceding code, we have used the `/by/admin` path in our API to differentiate this API from the customer's update method. Also, we get severity and status parameters from the request. Once the admin is validated by token, we will call the `updateTicket` method. If you see this `updateTicket` method, we haven't hard-coded anything.

Once the update process is done, we return the result "success" as a response, which you can check in the screenshot:

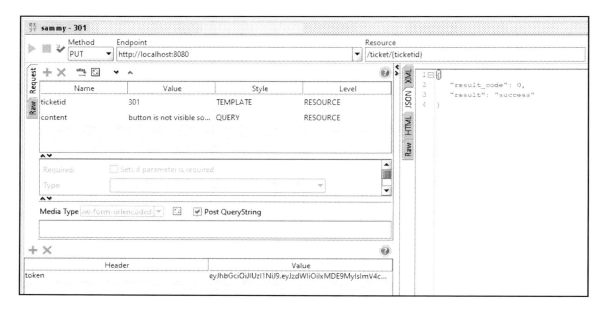

 In real applications, admin might not have control over customers' content, such as problems. However, we have provided an option for admin to edit the content to make our business logic easy.

Allowing admin to view a single ticket

As admin has full control of a ticket, they can also view any single ticket created by users. As we have already defined the getTicket API /{ticketid}, we can use the same API for admin viewing purposes as well.

Allowing admin to delete tickets

As admin has more control, we have given an unlimited multi-delete option for admin to delete in the application. This will be very handy when admin needs to delete a bunch of tickets in one shot.

Deleting tickets – service (TicketServiceImpl):

In the following code we will talk about multiple ticket delete option by admin:

```
@Override
public void deleteTickets(User user, String ticketids) {
  List<String> ticketObjList = Arrays.asList(ticketids.split(","));
  List<Integer> intList =
    ticketObjList.stream()
    .map(Integer::valueOf)
    .collect(Collectors.toList());
  tickets.removeIf(x -> intList.contains(x.getTicketid()));
}
```

In the preceding code, we have given admin the power to delete multiple tickets. As admin has full control, there are no specific filters we applied here. We use Java Streams to get tickets as list and then match them with ticket ID to delete from the ticket list.

Deleting tickets by admin – API (ticket controller):

The following method will forward the `ticketids` to the corresponding `TicketServiceImpl` method:

```
@ResponseBody
@AdminTokenRequired
@RequestMapping(value = "/by/admin", method = RequestMethod.DELETE)
public <T> T deleteTicketsByAdmin (
    @RequestParam("ticketids") final String ticketids,
    HttpServletRequest request
    ) {
  User user = userSevice.getUserByToken(request.getHeader("token"));
  ticketSevice.deleteTickets(user, ticketids);
  return Util.getSuccessResult();
}
```

In the preceding code, we first check the session by `@AdminTokenRequired` and then delete the ticket once the session is validated.

Ticket Management – Advanced CRUD

We can check the API result with this SoapUI screenshot:

In the multiple-ticket-delete option, we have used comma separated values to send multiple ticket IDs. A single `ticketid` also can be used to call this API.

CSR Ticket management

Finally, we will talk about CSR Ticket management in this section. CSR may not have controls like admin; however, in most cases, they have an option to match admin in Ticket management application. In the following section, we will talk about all CSR authorized CRUD operations on a ticket.

CSR updates a ticket

In this section, we will talk about updating a ticket by CSR with new content, severity, and status in Ticket management:

```
@ResponseBody
@CSRTokenRequired
@RequestMapping(value = "/by/csr", method = RequestMethod.PUT)
```

[198]

```java
public <T> T updateTicketByCSR (
    @RequestParam("ticketid") final Integer ticketid,
    @RequestParam(value="content") String content,
    @RequestParam(value="severity") Integer severity,
    @RequestParam(value="status") Integer status,
    HttpServletRequest request
    ) {
  ticketSevice.updateTicket(ticketid, content, severity, status);
  return Util.getSuccessResult();
}
```

In the preceding code, we get all the necessary information, such as content, severity, and status, and supply this information to the `updateTicket` method.

We have used a simple AOP for validating the admin token called `@CSRTokenRequired`. Let's look at the implementation part of this API.

CSRTokenRequired AOP

The `AdminTokenRequired` interface will be the base for our implementation that we will go through later:

```java
package com.packtpub.aop;
import java.lang.annotation.ElementType;
import java.lang.annotation.Retention;
import java.lang.annotation.RetentionPolicy;
import java.lang.annotation.Target;
@Retention(RetentionPolicy.RUNTIME)
@Target(ElementType.METHOD)
public @interface CSRTokenRequired {
}
```

In the preceding code, we introduced the annotation for validating admin token. The validation method will follow up in the `CSRTokenRequiredAspect` class.

CSRTokenRequiredAspect

In the `CSRTokenRequiredAspect` class, we will do the validation of admin token:

```java
package com.packtpub.aop;
import javax.servlet.http.HttpServletRequest;
import javax.xml.bind.DatatypeConverter;
import org.aspectj.lang.annotation.Aspect;
import org.aspectj.lang.annotation.Before;
```

```
import org.springframework.stereotype.Component;
import org.springframework.util.StringUtils;
import org.springframework.web.context.request.RequestContextHolder;
import org.springframework.web.context.request.ServletRequestAttributes;
import com.packtpub.service.SecurityServiceImpl;
import io.jsonwebtoken.Claims;
import io.jsonwebtoken.Jwts;
@Aspect
@Component
public class CSRTokenRequiredAspect {
  @Before("@annotation(csrTokenRequired)")
  public void adminTokenRequiredWithAnnotation(CSRTokenRequired csrTokenRequired) throws Throwable{
    ServletRequestAttributes reqAttributes = (ServletRequestAttributes)RequestContextHolder.currentRequestAttributes();
    HttpServletRequest request = reqAttributes.getRequest();
    // checks for token in request header
    String tokenInHeader = request.getHeader("token");
    if(StringUtils.isEmpty(tokenInHeader)){
      throw new IllegalArgumentException("Empty token");
    }
    Claims claims = Jwts.parser()
.setSigningKey(DatatypeConverter.parseBase64Binary(SecurityServiceImpl.secretKey))
            .parseClaimsJws(tokenInHeader).getBody();
    if(claims == null || claims.getSubject() == null){
      throw new IllegalArgumentException("Token Error : Claim is null");
    }
    String subject = claims.getSubject();
    if(subject.split("=").length != 2 || new Integer(subject.split("=")[1]) != 2){
      throw new IllegalArgumentException("User is not authorized");
    }
  }
}
```

In the preceding code, we have provided the token validation technique in our `CSRTokenRequiredAspect` class. This aspect component will be executed before the method execution. Also, in this method, we check the token for empty and null as well as the user type of the token.

Here's the screenshot of our /ticket/{ticketid} update API:

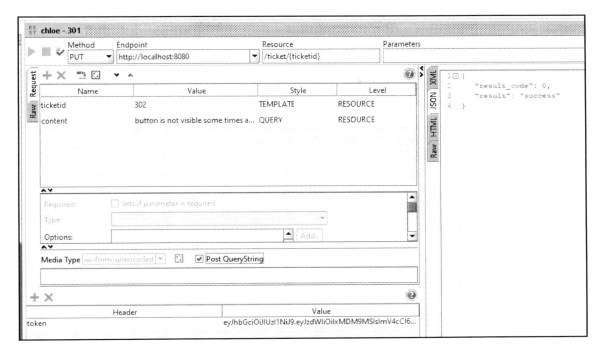

CSR view all tickets

In terms of viewing all tickets, CSR has the same rights as admin, so we don't need to change the service implementation. However, we may need to validate the token to ensure that the user is CSR.

Viewing all tickets by CSR – API (ticket controller)

The following will get all the tickets for CSR when it's called by any CSR:

```
@ResponseBody
@CSRTokenRequired
@RequestMapping("/by/csr")
public <T> T getAllTicketsByCSR(HttpServletRequest request) {
    return (T) ticketSevice.getAllTickets();
}
```

Ticket Management – Advanced CRUD

In the preceding API, we have used only `@CSRTokenRequired` to validate the user. Everything other than the API path and annotation is the same, as admin views all the tickets.

When we check the screenshot of SoapUI, we can clearly see two tickets created by customers.

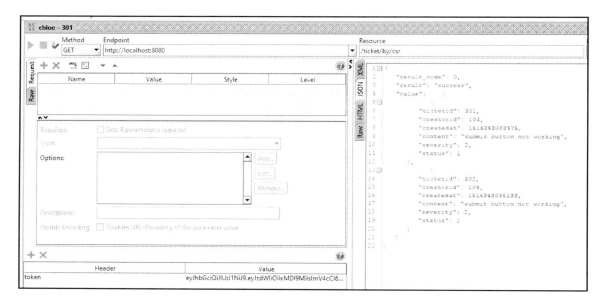

CSR view single ticket

Other than the multi-delete option, CSR has equal rights as admin, we can use the same `/{ticketid}`, which we used for both CSR and admin view single ticket API here.

CSR delete tickets

Deleting tickets by CSR is almost like deleting tickets in admin mode. However, our business requirements say that CSR should not be able to delete more than three tickets at a time. We will add the specific logic to our existing method.

Deleting tickets – service (TicketServivceImpl)

Here comes the service implementation for deleting multiple tickets by CSR:

```
@Override
public void deleteTickets(User user, String ticketids) {
   List<String> ticketObjList = Arrays.asList(ticketids.split(","));
   if(user.getUsertype() == 2 && ticketObjList.size() > 3){
      throw new RuntimeException("CSR can't delete more than 3 tickets");
   }
   List<Integer> intList =
     ticketObjList.stream()
     .map(Integer::valueOf)
     .collect(Collectors.toList())
       ;
   tickets.removeIf(x -> intList.contains(x.getTicketid()));
}
```

For deleting multi-tickets, we have used the existing code in the `TicketServiceImpl` class. However, as per our business requirements, our CSR can't delete more than three tickets, so we have added extra logic to check the ticket size. If the ticket list size is more than three, we throw an exception, otherwise we will remove those tickets.

Deleting tickets by CSR – API (ticket controller)

In the API, we will simply call the `deleteTickets` method that we implemented earlier:

```
@ResponseBody
@CSRTokenRequired
@RequestMapping(value = "/by/csr", method = RequestMethod.DELETE)
public <T> T deleteTicketsByCSR (
    @RequestParam("ticketids") final String ticketids,
    HttpServletRequest request,
    HttpServletResponse response
   ) {
  User user = userSevice.getUserByToken(request.getHeader("token"));
  ticketSevice.deleteTickets(user.getUserid(), ticketids);
  Map<String, String> result = new LinkedHashMap<>();
  result.put("result", "deleted");
  return (T) result;
}
```

Other than the max ticket restriction on the delete option, there is no big change needed for CSR to delete tickets. However, we have added the `@CSRTokenRequired` annotation used in our API.

Ticket Management – Advanced CRUD

This is the screenshot of SoapUI for CSR deletes multiple tickets:

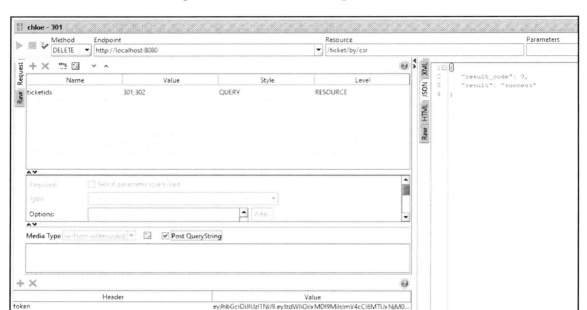

 The Postman tool may have an issue with the DELETE option, including parameters (as of version 5.4.0), you may not get the expected results when you use multiple-delete API in both admin and CSR. For such scenarios, please use SoapUI client.

Summary

In this final chapter, we have implemented a small Ticket Management System by meeting all the business requirements that we mentioned in the first section of this chapter. This implementation covers ticket CRUD operations by customer, CSR, and admin. Also, our implementation met the business requirements, such as why CSR can't delete more than three tickets at a time.

Other Books You May Enjoy

If you enjoyed this book, you may be interested in these other books by Packt:

Spring 5.0 Microservices - Second Edition

Rajesh R V

ISBN: 978-1-78712-768-5

- Familiarize yourself with the microservices architecture and its benefits
- Find out how to avoid common challenges and pitfalls while developing microservices
- Use Spring Boot and Spring Cloud to develop microservices
- Handle logging and monitoring microservices
- Leverage Reactive Programming in Spring 5.0 to build modern cloud native applications
- Manage internet-scale microservices using Docker, Mesos, and Marathon
- Gain insights into the latest inclusion of Reactive Streams in Spring and make applications more resilient and scalable

Other Books You May Enjoy

Mastering Spring 5.0

Ranga Karanam

ISBN: 978-1-78712-317-5

- Explore the new features in Spring Framework 5.0
- Build microservices with Spring Boot
- Get to know the advanced features of Spring Boot in order to effectively develop and monitor applications
- Use Spring Cloud to deploy and manage applications on the Cloud
- Understand Spring Data and Spring Cloud Data Flow
- Understand the basics of reactive programming
- Get to know the best practices when developing applications with the Spring Framework
- Create a new project using Kotlin and implement a couple of basic services with unit and integration testing

Leave a review - let other readers know what you think

Please share your thoughts on this book with others by leaving a review on the site that you bought it from. If you purchased the book from Amazon, please leave us an honest review on this book's Amazon page. This is vital so that other potential readers can see and use your unbiased opinion to make purchasing decisions, we can understand what our customers think about our products, and our authors can see your feedback on the title that they have worked with Packt to create. It will only take a few minutes of your time, but is valuable to other potential customers, our authors, and Packt. Thank you!

Index

A

admin login
  creating 177
admin ticket management
  about 191
  ticket view access, providing to admin 191
Aerospike
  reference 152
AOP (@Before) execution
  about 126
  testing 127
AOP (@Before) with annotation
  about 128
  testing 129
Apache Maven
  about 15
  reference 15
  used, for creating project 17
application-tier caching
  about 150
  Aerospike 152
  Cache2k 152
  Ehcache 151
  Hazelcast 151
  Infinispan 152
  Memcached 150
  Redis 151
  Riak 151
aspect-oriented programming (AOP)
  about 125
  AOP (@Before) execution 126
  AOP (@Before) with annotation 127
  integrating, with JWT 129

C

cache implementation
  about 116
  ETags, using 121, 124
  REST resource, using 116, 120
cache validation
  about 115
  ETags 115
  Last-Modified/If-Modified-Since headers 115
Cache2k
  reference 152
clustering
  about 145
  benefits 146
  scaling out (horizontal scaling) 146
  scaling up (vertical scaling) 146
content negotiation
  about 110
  Accept-Encoding 110
  agent-driven content negotiation 112
  Content-Encoding 111
  server-driven content negotiation 111
createUser
  endpoint, testing 57
  implementation, in handler and repository 56
CRUD operations
  createUser 56
  createUser implementation 76
  deleteUser 61, 62
  deleteUser implementation 80
  getAllUsers 51
  getAllUsers implementation 73
  getUser 54
  getUser implementation 75
  HTTP methods 48
  in Spring 5 71

mapping, to HTTP methods 66
Reactive server initialization 49
sample values, in repository 50
updateUser 58
updateUser implementation 78
used, for ticket management 167
CSR login 179
CSR ticket management
  about 198
  all tickets, viewing 201
  API (ticket controller) 201, 203
  CSRTokenRequired AOP 199
  CSRTokenRequiredAspect 199
  service (TicketServivceImpl) 203
  single ticket, viewing 202
  ticket updation, by CSR 198
  tickets, deleting 202
customer login
  creating 176
customer service representative (CSR) 13, 167

D

data-tier caching
  about 149
  first-level caching 150
  second-level caching 150
database partitioning
  about 148
  sharding (horizontal partitioning) 149
  vertical partitioning 149
database, scaling
  about 147
  database partitioning 148
  horizontal scaling 147
  load balancing, in DB servers 148
  multiple masters, using 148
  pool connections 148
  read replicas 147
  vertical scaling 147
deleteUser
  endpoint, testing 62
  implementing, in handler and repository 61
dependency trees 22
distributed caching
  about 149, 152

Amazon ElastiCache 152
application-tier caching 150
data-tier caching 149
Oracle distributed cache (Coherence) 152

E

Eclipse MicroProfile 164
Ehcache
  reference 151
Elastic Load Balancer (ELB) 161
error handling
  about 141
  customized exception 143

F

F5
  reference 146
file uploads
  REST API 80
  testing 83
Flux 36

G

getAllUsers
  endpoint, testing 53
  implementation, in handler 52
  mapping 51
getUser
  endpoint, testing 56
  implementation, in handler 54

H

HAProxy
  reference 146
HashiCorp Consul 164
Hazelcast
  reference 151
horizontal scaling 147
HTTP cache control
  no-cache 113
  only-if-cached 114
  private caching 113
  public caching 112
HTTP caching

about 112
  cache control 112
  cache validation 115
HTTP compression
  about 109
  content negotiation 110
HTTP methods
  CRUD operations, mapping to 66
Hypermedia as the Engine of Application State
    (HATEOAS) 8

I

imperative programming 10
Infinispan
  reference 152

J

Java Cryptography Architecture (JCA) 88
Java Util Logging (JUL) 133
Java
  Reactive programming 12
JavaScript Object Notation (JSON) 7
JSON Web Token (JWT)
  about 85, 86
  AOP, integrating with 129
  dependency 86
jsoup
  about 104
  test cases, executing 108
  user, adding 107
  user, obtaining 106
JUnit
  about 93
  jsoup 104
  MockMVC 94
  Postman 97
  SoapUI 100
JWT token
  subject, obtaining from 90

L

load balancing 146
Log4j 2.9.1
  adding, to POM dependency 20

Logback
  dependency and configuration 133
  framework 132
  implementation in class 134
logger controls
  about 132
  Log4J 132
  Logback 132
  SLF4J 132
login
  about 175
  admin login 177
  CSR login 179
  customer login 176

M

microservice components
  circuit breaker 160
  configuration server 159
  edge server 160
  load balancer 159
  service discovery 160
microservice tools
  about 161
  Eclipse MicroProfile 164
  HashiCorp Consul 164
  Netflix Hystrix 163
  Netflix Ribbon 162
  Netflix Turbine 164
  Netflix Zuul 161
  Spring Cloud Netflix 162
microservice
  about 156
  automated environment 157
  autonomy 157
  benefits 158
  components 159
  resilience and fault tolerance 157
  stateless 158
  tools 160
MockMVC
  about 94
  single user, testing 95
Mono 37
monolithic

architecture 155
drawbacks 155

N

Netflix Eureka 161
Netflix Hystrix
  about 163
  circuit breaker fallback mechanism 163
Netflix Ribbon 162
Netflix Turbine 164
Netflix Zuul 161

O

Open Source Software (OSS) 162

P

Plain Old Java Object (POJO) 36
POM dependency
  Log4j 2.9.1, adding 20
POM file
  viewing, post to project creation 17
Postman
  about 58, 97
  JWT, generating 99
  subject, obtaining from token 99
  user, adding 98
  users, obtaining 97
Project Object Model (POM)
  dependencies 19
  file structure 18

R

Reactive Core 34
Reactive programming
  about 10
  benefits 11, 33
  in Java 12
  in Spring 5 12
  user class, using with 37, 41
Reactive Streams (RS)
  about 11, 34, 37
  and back pressures 35
Redis
  reference 151

registration
  about 168
  admin registration 172
  CSR registration 174
  customer registration 170
Representational State Transfer (REST)
  about 7, 8, 10
  cacheable 9
  client and server 8
  code on demand (COD) 9
  layered system 9
  stateless 8
  uniform interface 8
resources
  creating 66, 71
REST API 36
REST client
  building 137
  RestTemplate 138, 140
RESTful web services
  architecture 12
  developing 24
  favorite IDE, working with 26, 30
  project base, creating 24
Riak
  reference 151

S

server-sent-event (SSE) 164
Simple Mail Transfer Protocol (SMTP) 7
Simple Object Access Protocol (SOAP) 7
Single Sign On (SSO) 86
single ticket
  viewing by admin 196
SLF4j
  logging levels 134
SoapUI
  about 58, 100
  JWT SoapUI, generating 102
  subject, obtaining from token 103
  users, obtaining 101
Spring 5
  Reactive programming 12
Spring Boot 24
Spring Cloud Netflix 162

Spring Initializr
  reference 24, 66
Spring REST
  CRUD operations 47
Spring Security
  about 85
  authentication 86
  authorization 86
  JSON Web Token (JWT) 86
  JWT token, creating 87
  subject, getting from JWT token 90
  subject, getting from token 91
  token, generating 89
Spring Tool Suite (STS)
  reference 26

T

throwSecure Hash Algorithm (SHA) 88
Ticket Management System 12
ticket management
  about 180
  CRUD operations, using 167
  single ticket, viewing 187
  ticket POJO 180
  ticket updation, by ticket 188
  ticket, deleting 189
  tickets, obtaining from counter 186
  User Ticket management 182
ticket POJO
  about 180
  user, obtaining by token 181
ticket
  deleting 190, 197
  deleting, by admin 196, 197
  service, deleting in TicketServiceImpl 190
  updating, by admin 195
  updating, TicketServiceImpl class 188
token
  generating 175
  management 175

U

Uniform Resource Identifier (URI) 8
universally unique identifier (UUIDs) 148
updateUser
  endpoint, testing 60
  implementing, in handler and repository 58
user class
  using, with Reactive programming 37, 41
user POJO 168, 170
User Ticket management
  about 182
  ticket controller 182
  UserTokenRequired interface 183
  UserTokenRequiredAspect class 184
user types 168

V

vertical scaling 147
view ticket method
  AdminTokenRequired interface 192
  AdminTokenRequiredAspect class 193
  API (ticket controller) 192
  service (TicketServiceImpl) 192

W

WebFlux 35

24291385R00130

Printed in Poland
by Amazon Fulfillment
Poland Sp. z o.o., Wrocław